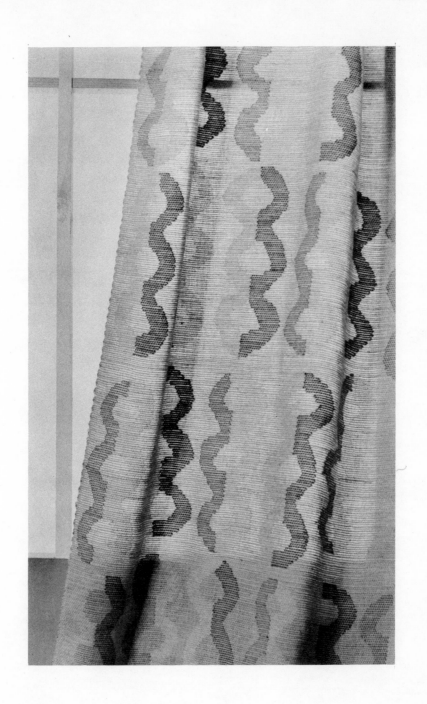

MANUAL OF
SWEDISH
HAND WEAVING

By ULLA CYRUS

Translation by
Viola Anderson

Charles T. Branford Company
Boston, Massachusetts

1956

Printed in The United States of America

CONTENTS

vi

WEAVING AND WEAVING EQUIPMENT

SETTING UP THE LOOM

Preparation of the warp

The first step in weaving is to prepare the *warp*, calculating its length and the number of threads required for its width. The warp yarn should be orderly so that it will unreel smoothly. Yarns in skeins should be *wound* on spools. Colored yarns usually come put up in skeins, since it is difficult to dye them evenly on tubes. This is especially true of sunfast and washable yarns.

Certain yarns are sized in order to withstand strain during weaving.

Before the warp can be beamed it must be spread out to its full width. This process is called preliminary sleying or *pre-sleying*.

The following equipment is needed to prepare a warp: swift, winding reel and spools, warping reel, reed and reed hook.

Sizing of yarns. Certain yarns require sizing which cannot withstand wear against heddles or reeds or which have long loose fibres that are likely to catch into each other. Examples of such yarns are cotton singles, bleached or linen singles, wool singles loosely spun, or yarns of extremely fine quality. In general, handweaving yarns do not need to be sized. Cotton yarns are usually of two or more ply, and singles in linen and wool are especially prepared for warping. Warp-spun yarns contain more twists per centimeter than weft-spun yarns and often have been dipped in a solution to further strengthen them. Fully bleached linen yarns are not recommended for handweaving since they are not so durable and are less attractive than quarter and semi-bleached yarns. Dyed linen

9

singles become less durable through the bleaching and dyeing processes and should be sized when used for warp. Extremely fine twisted linen yarns may also be sized.

Sizing of linen yarns. The gluten in linseed may be used as a sizing. Linseed is boiled in water to a thick consistency, after which the seeds are strained out and the solution allowed to cool. The yarn skeins are tied loosely in a couple of places to prevent tangling and are dipped in the sizing mixture. Press out any excess sizing and hang the skeins up to dry. While the yarn is still damp wind it on spools, passing the strands back and forth to spread them out and allow them to dry. By winding the yarns while still damp, the fibres will lie close to the strands. Linen yarns may also be sized with wheat flour to which paraffin has been added. For $4\frac{1}{2}$ pounds of linen yarn take 6 quarts of water, $5\frac{1}{4}$ ounces of flour and $1\frac{3}{4}$ ounces of paraffin. Boil the water and flour; remove from heat; add the paraffin and beat until the mixture cools. Size the skeins in the same way as with the linseed solution.

The warp may also be sized on the loom by using the above solution. Care should be taken not to allow the reed to rust. Using two soft brushes apply the sizing to both sides of that section of the warp which has been drawn forward on the loom. If the warp is sized in the afternoon, it will be dry by the following morning.

Cool damp rooms are best for linen warps, and the warp should not be exposed to strong sunlight. The warp may be kept damp by placing a pan of water under the warp beam, or a wet cloth may be thoroughly wrung out and placed on the beam. Warm, damp rooms are most suitable for wool and cotton warps.

Winding of skeins. The skein to be wound is placed on a *swift* (Fig. 1), which should be in a horizontal position. The one in the illustration is constructed in such a way that the skein may be spread out on crossbars parallel to the axle.

Before the skein is placed on the swift, it should be shaken out well between the hands or may be placed over a round stick, in order to even out the strands. The skein is then spread out on

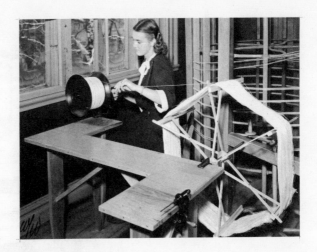

Fig. 1. Winding.

the swift in orderly arrangement according to divisional skein string.
The end strand of yarn is attached to the end of the skein string,
which should be cut but not drawn out of the skein. If a strand of
yarn should break and not be found, the skein may be divided with
the aid of the skein string, and in this way the end strand will
appear.

The winding reel with the large spool, seen in the illustration, is
a very good one and takes up very little space. It resembles a
large bobbin winder and may also be used for winding large-size
bobbins. The spools are made of metal with flanges at each end.
There are also wooden spools which are used on a reel having an
axle with connecting crank that is turned by hand, or with a treadle
arrangement.

The winding reel should be placed so that the yarn runs straight
from the swift to the spool. The amount of yarn to be used in the
warp should be divided evenly on each spool. A linen warp is
usually warped from two spools, while a cotton warp may have
four. On the metal spool the thread is wound by passing it back
and forth across the whole width of the spool. But when using the
large wooden spool, begin winding the yarn at the widest end of

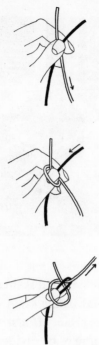

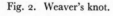

Fig. 3. Warping.

Fig. 2. Weaver's knot.

the spool, filling about 6 inches at a time. The threads are spliced using the weaver's knot and the ends neatly trimmed off.

The *weaver's knot* is made in the following manner (Fig. 2).

I. Place the first thread between the thumb and forefinger of the left hand (the heavy black line in the illustration) and the second thread in back of the first.

II. With the second thread make a loop around the thumb, in back of the second end, and over the first end.

III. With the right hand fold the first end over and through the loop held in the left hand. Then take the second thread in the right hand and pull to tighten the knot.

When warping with more than four threads it is better to wind the yarn on smaller spools. These spools are wound on a bobbin

12

winder (see illustration) or on a spinning wheel. In the latter case, the spools will require a groove on one side for the spinning wheel cord, if there is no provision for this on the wheel.

Warping. A warping reel of the usual type is shown in Fig. 3. The warping reel, with its vertical axis placed in a stand, carries at the top and at the bottom crossed boards which are notched at their centers to permit folding when not in use. Four vertical staves are attached to these crossed boards. A detachable board with two or three lease pegs is placed at the lower end of the reel between two of the staves. Each stave contains several holes for the end peg.

The circumference of the warping reel is measured. In the reel illustrated, the distance between the staves is $2\frac{1}{2}$ feet and the circumference is thus almost 10 feet. The distance from the stave to the last lease peg is 20–24 inches. A warp which is 14 feet 11 inches, i.e., 15 revolutions, may easily be wound on this reel without any danger of turns of warp lengths coming too close to each other.

In estimating the length of the warp, consideration must be given to the distance between each of the staves of the warping reel. Thus, when the warp length has been calculated, it will be necessary to compare its measurements to the warping reel's measurements, and in the final analysis the length may have to be altered slightly to adjust to the reel.

Example:

	ft.	in.		ft.	in.
I. Estim. warp length	40	0	4 revolutions (3 × 4)	39	4
Added warp length		10	lease . . .		20
Warp length	40	10		41	0
II. Estim. warp length	33	11	3 revolutions (3 × 3)	29	6
Subtracted length		4	1 section on reel .	2	6
			lease . . .		20
Warp length	33	7		33	7

13

When *warping*, the large spools of warp yarn are placed on the floor, with guide rings for the threads placed above them. A simple method is to use curtain rings, one for each spool, fastened to a cord stretched above the spools. However, if the warp yarn is on small spools or on tubes, these should be placed on a spool rack.

When the number of revolutions of the reel have been determined, place the end peg in the proper hole of the stave which is to be the starting point of the warp. Tie the threads together and loop them over this peg. Turn the reel with the left hand, and with the right lay the threads on the staves in a spiral down toward the *lease*. The purpose of the lease is to keep the threads in correct order. In forming the lease, lay the threads over the first peg, under the second and third peg, and then back over the third and second and under the first. In returning upwards in this first revolution, place the threads about $1\frac{1}{2}$ inches below the previously warped threads. One complete circuit of the warp on the reel is called a *bout*.

Warping continues, always placing the threads above the threads of the previous revolution in the downward direction and below the threads in the upward direction. Now and then the threads should be *pushed together* so that they do not spread out too much.

The threads should be counted at the lease where they have been laid in correct order. Down at the last lease peg the bouts may be drawn together, as for example $10 + 10 + 5 = 25$ bouts. When warping with two threads each bout will contain 4 threads, and 25 bouts 100 threads. Check the count of every 100 threads and separate each group with a twist of string.

When threads of different kinds are required in the warp, the change should be made either at the end peg or at the lease. In this instance the threads being warped are cut off and the new thread or threads are tied to the original ones.

It is always advisable to make a complete warp without any interruptions and by the same person throughout the entire process. In instances of very wide warps of many threads, these may be

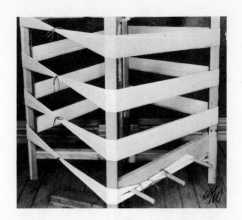

Fig. 4. Tying of the warp.

divided into two or more sections. For example, a warp of more than 3 feet 3 inches in width should be divided into two or more sections, depending on its full width. If a warp contains yarns of differing degrees of elasticity, as for example a warp for double weave using wool and linen, each type of yarn should be warped separately and combined in the pre-sleying process.

When the warp has been completed, tie the lease as in Fig. 4. First tie a cord around the groups of threads separated by each of the two lease pegs, in order to retain the lease. Tie another cord around the warp about 2¾ feet from the lease. The cords should,

Fig. 5. Warping with a paddle.

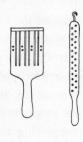

Fig. 6. Paddles.

15

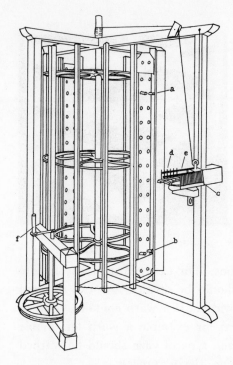

Fig. 7. Warp.

at this place, be wound around the warp several times and tied firmly with a bow knot. By tying the warp firmly, the threads will not become tangled or out of order during the pre-sleying. Continue to tie the warp once for each revolution and at the end peg. If the warp is divided into several sections, it is preferable to tie the warp at each stave. Thus in each section the cords will come in exactly the same places, and when beaming the warp it will aid in keeping the same tension for all of the sections.

Now the warp is ready to be *chained*. Beginning at the top, hold the warp firmly, and pull out the end peg. Using the loop which was formed at the end peg, pull the warp through to make a new loop. Continue in this manner, *alternatingly* drawing the warp through the loops formed first with the right hand and then with the left, completing the chain at the tied section nearest the lease (30 inches from the lease). At this point tie the last loop using the same cord. Do not pull the end of the warp through this last loop.

Fig. 8. Lease.

When *warping with several threads simultaneously*, there should be two leases. In the first lease, which is made at the bottom of the reel, all of the threads are held together as a unit, and are the basis of the order of threads in pre-sleying. This lease is called the *beaming lease*. In the second lease, which is made at the upper section of the reel, one or two threads only are held together. This is called the *threading lease* and is used in threading the warp.

This type of warp may be made on an ordinary warping reel with the assistance of a *paddle* and an additional crossboard with lease pegs (Fig. 5). In this case, one crossboard is placed at the upper end and the other at the lower end of the warping reel. The threads are then threaded through the paddle, which is held in the right hand, while the threads are guided by the left hand.

The beaming lease is laid in the usual way and the threading lease is made on the upper lease pegs with the help of the paddle. Fig. 6 shows two types of paddles. When using the paddle seen on the left, the lease is made by first raising the paddle and then lowering it. Using the paddle on the right, however, the threads from one row of holes lie over the thumb, while those from the other row lie the forefinger. When the warping has been completed both leases are tied properly, and all other sections of the warp are tied as described earlier. The warp is then chained down with the beginning at the threading lease.

17

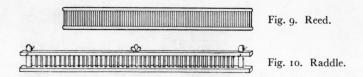

Fig. 9. Reed.

Fig. 10. Raddle.

Fig. 7 shows a *large warping reel*, suitable for a studio or workshop. This reel has an arrangement which, as it turns, automatically lays the threads in a spiral at regular distances between each revolution. It has a circumference of 13 feet 1 inch, and twenty revolutions or 262 feet may be warped.

The threading lease is placed in the upper area at *a*, and the beaming lease in the lower at *b*. In place of the paddle there are two combs *c*. The teeth of the combs have eyes through which the threads are drawn. In order to make the lease (Fig. 8), lift the first comb and place the middle finger between the threads. Next raise the second comb and insert the forefinger through the threads. Alternating threads should thus lie over the two fingers. In this way the lease is carried to the lease pegs on the reel. To keep the threads in position, they are placed in the dents *d* and held in place by the clamp *e*. The reel is turned by means of the lever *f*.

Pre-sleying. To pre-sley, the warp *bouts* are drawn through an ordinary reed or placed in a raddle. The purpose of the pre-sleying reed is to spread out the warp to its full width while it is being beamed on the loom. When beaming has been completed, the reed is removed. The warp is then threaded through the heddles and the warp finally sleyed. If there is sufficient space on the warp beam, the pre-sleyed width should be about 5% wider than the reeding width. This added width on the yarn beam makes it easier to hold out the warp during weaving.

Reeds, Fig. 9, are now made of steel. The number or set of a reed is usually labeled at one end. (Example: 100–10–100. The reed has 100 dents to 4 inches and is 3 feet 3 inches long. The Swedish word "rör" derives from the time when reeds were made of bamboo.)

Raddles, Fig. 10, are made of steel or wood. The set of the raddle is never as close as that of the reed used in the weaving. The upper crossbar of the raddle may be removed so that the bouts may be placed in the dents.

Pre-sleying. The reed to be used for pre-sleying should have a set which will allow one bout to be drawn through each dent. The bouts cannot be divided. Generally a raddle which would permit the exact number to be pre-sleyed is not available and it will be necessary to figure out the best possible set for the reed at hand.

In general, the pre-sleying reed has a set which is half as close as the weaving reed. The weaving reed is often threaded with two threads in each dent, but in warping there are usually four threads in a bout. A weaving reed with 100 dents to 4 inches should then be replaced by a pre-sleying reed of 50 dents to 4 inches. Bearing in mind that the width of the warp in the pre-sleying reed should be somewhat greater than the width in the weaving reed, allowance should be made by leaving extra empty dents at regular intervals. This is, of course, in the event that one does not have a coarser reed, as for example, a reed of 48 dents to 4 inches.

Example: Warping with 2 threads, total number of threads 1,280, reed 100/2 (100 dents to 4 inches, 2 threads in each dent, 20 threads per $\frac{3}{8}$ inch).

No. of threads in 1 bout	4	No. of bouts (1,280 ÷ 4)	320
Weaving reed width		Pre-sleying reed width	
(1,280 ÷ 20) . .	25 in.	(64 + 5%) . .	26½ in.

I. Since one bout is drawn through each dent, the number of bouts and dents in the pre-sleying width will be the same. The set is thus computed by dividing the number of dents by the width of the pre-sleying width.

No. of dents .	. .	.	320
Pre-sleying reed (320 ÷ 6.7) .	.		48 dents per 4 in.

Threading: 1 bout in each dent.

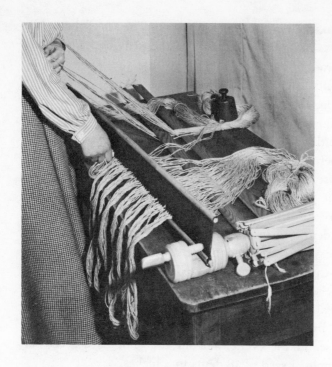

Fig. 11. Pre-sleying.

II. If only the weaving reed is available, one bout may be drawn through every other dent, leaving a few extra empty dents in the pre-sleying width. In calculating this threading, the total number of dents in the pre-sleying width is divided by the number of bouts, the remaining dents then being distributed evenly according to a certain number of bouts.

Pre-sleying reed .   .   .   .   100 dents per 4 in.

No. of dents in 26½ in. .   .   .   670

Threading: 1 bout in every other dent, and after 10 bouts, skip an extra dent.

Check: 1 in. 25 dents and 12 bouts.

III. Frequently the only reed available for the pre-sleying is of an entirely different set. In this case the threading can be worked out by comparing the number of dents with the number of bouts. If there are many more dents than bouts, it will be necessary to skip a certain number of dents, while if there are more bouts, some of these will have to be doubled in the dents.

No. of bouts 320

Possible pre-sleying reed . . 35 dents per 4 in.

No. of dents per $26\frac{1}{2}$ in. . . 235

Threading: 1 bout in a dent, 2 bouts in every third dent.

$(320 \div 235 = 1$ with a remainder of 85

$235 \div 85 =$ approx. 3)

Check: 4 in. 35 dents and 47 bouts.

When a raddle is used, the calculations are worked out in the same way as for a reed.

Fig. 12. Warp beam.

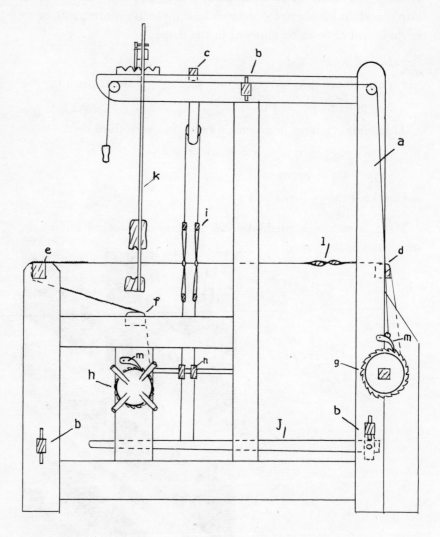

Fig. 13. Loom.

However, with a raddle it is also possible to lay half bouts in the dents.

Example: Warping with 10 threads, total number of threads 1,280, pre-sleying width 67 centimeters.

No. of threads in bout   .   20

No. of bouts   .   .   64 whole or 128 half bouts

Raddle (64 ÷ 6.7)   .   .   9.6, which is raised to 10

Threading: 1 whole bout in each dent for 19 bouts, then skip one dent. A better plan is to lay one-half bout in each dent in a 20 dent raddle and then skip one dent after 19 half bouts.

The process of pre-sleying may be carried out on a table, at a loom, or at a special stand. Fig. 11 shows sleying on a table.

Insert two lease sticks through both leases and tie the sticks about $2\frac{3}{4}$ inches apart. The warp chain is then fastened securely at the table or a heavy weight placed on it at the first firmly tied knot. The width is measured on the reed, and the reed hook is placed in the beginning dent. The first hundred threads are separated from the others as far as to the first firmly tied knot. The bouts are then taken in order at the lease and by means of the reed hook are drawn through the dents. When the first group of bouts have been drawn in, a stick is passed through them or they may be twisted together so that they do not slip out of the reed. When the threading has been completed, the width should be checked for accuracy.

When a raddle is used, place the lease sticks in front of the raddle. The bouts are laid in the dents, after which the upper bar is fitted on and tied.

The warp on the loom

When the pre-sleying has been completed, the warp is ready to be wound on the warp beam of the loom. This process is called *beaming*. The warp is then *threaded*. In other words, the threads are drawn through the eyes of the heddles which are on the harnesses.

The warp is once again drawn through the reed, after which it is tied forward on the rod attached by cords to the cloth beam. The essentials required for the warp are thus: the loom itself, the heddles, the reed and the reed hook.

Description of the loom. A present-day Swedish loom (counterbalanced loom) of the usual type may be seen in Fig. 13, and includes the following parts:

The frame, which consists of two side supports *a*, held in position by three crossbars *b*; detachable parts such as the crossbar with the attachments for hanging the heddle frames, or harnesses *c*, the back beam *d*, the breast beam *e*, the knee beam *f*, and the bench; movable parts, such as the warp beam *g*, the cloth beam *h*, the harnesses *i*, the treadles *j*, the beater *k*, and the lease sticks *l*. The warp beam and the cloth beam are controlled by the wheels and ratchets *m*. Between the harnesses and treadles are the lamms *n* (more clearly seen in Fig. 27).

Of the above-mentioned parts the back beam, the knee beam and the lamms are often not found on older looms.

A loom should be well proportioned and each part carefully constructed in order to fulfill its function most effectively. The side supports should be high enough (about 60 inches) to allow sufficient room for the upper tie-up. A high loom is also more satisfactory, as the beater gives a better stroke. The loom should be of sufficient length (about 55 inches) to provide a better shed and to lessen the strain on the warp. The side supports should be so constructed as to give the weaver easy access into the loom to tie up the treadles. The crossbars are secured to the side supports with wedges or are screwed in.

The advantage of the back beam is that the height of the warp remains the same and in addition, the warp will have a longer stretch, since the warp beam is then placed lower down between the side supports. The knee beam serves to raise the woven material, thus protecting it from the weaver's knees. The ratchets on the warp and cloth beams should be on the outer side of the loom in

24

order not to cut down the full weaving width. It is also practical to have the warp and cloth beams grooved, so that the rods holding the warp may be slipped into the beams. The cords are used only to pull the rods down to the beams and are then removed (Fig. 12). In contrast to older looms, the treadles are usually secured to the back crossbar.

The beater is suspended from the upper part of the loom. Since it easily gets out of alignment, the hanging arrangement should be such that it may be accurately adjusted. The beater is correctly hung when, by careful measurement, it is parallel to the breast beam. The illustration shows a wedge on the beater, which is placed in one of the notches on top of the side support. The wedge is in front of the beater sword, which causes the beater to incline toward the weave, thus adding weight to the beat. The groove in which the reed is placed is also in front of the beater swords, thus permitting the use of a reed which is longer than the beater itself.

Looms are usually constructed of pine. Beech or birch are best for the beater, and the wooden reed holder should be glued, so that it will not warp. Iron is frequently used for the wedges and grooves of the beater, but a hard wood is considered to be more satisfactory than metal.

The uprights holding the breast beam of the loom are exposed to particularly heavy strain and should, therefore, be reinforced.

Rug looms require unusually sturdy construction and should be provided with special devices for beaming and stretching the warp. The beams may be made of hard wood, steel cylinders, or wood-encased U-iron.

Assembling the loom. To assemble the loom, first stand the side supports upright and lay the crossbars between them. Marks, or numbers, on the side supports as well as on the beams indicate the correct positions of the crossbars and beams. The crossbars and beams which go in first should be eased into position in their proper places in the side supports. Any parts which do not go into place easily can be sandpapered down to fit, but they must not be

Fig. 14. Transferring the lease.

hammered in. When wedges are used to hold the crossbars in place, a wooden mallet may be used to hammer them down. However, if the crossbars are screwed in, washers should be put in between the wood and the bolts.

When the frame has been assembled, all other beams are slipped into place. Smaller parts like the heddle sticks, lamms, harness holders, etc., should be labeled with the number of the loom before being used.

To prevent the loom from "walking" during weaving, blocks may be fastened to the floor in front of the two uprights. Other suggestions for keeping the loom in place are to lay two boards

26

from the loom uprights to the opposite wall, or to place heavy rubber mats under the supports.

Beaming. Before the warp is put on the loom, the harnesses are disconnected from the treadles, rolled up and put aside. Beam sticks and selvedge papers are brought out. The beam sticks, which should be at least 2 inches longer than the pre-sleyed warp width, are used on the warp beam to separate the layers of warp. The purpose of the selvedge papers is to keep the outer warp threads from slipping over the edge and becoming slack. For selvedge papers, use heavy paper about 16 inches × 24 inches. Fold the paper lengthwise one-fourth in toward the center, and fold this section two more times. The paper now consists of one single section and one of eight thicknesses. Draw the paper over an edge

Fig. 15. Beaming with a raddle.

to make it pliable. About two selvedge papers are required for every 5 yards. Flanges may be used in place of selvedge papers.

Beaming the warp with one lease and with an ordinary reed as the pre-sley reed. The pre-sley reed is placed in the beater so that the warp is centered. The rod on the warp beam is drawn forward and inserted through the loops of warp, which should be evenly divided between the cords.

The warp may be held either in back or in front of the loom. In the former instance, it is carried around the breast beam and is held as far back of the loom as space permits, in this way making the tension more even. In the latter position, the warp is carried around the breast beam and the knee beam and is held in front of the loom. This way the warp goes around two beams and is more tightly stretched.

Two, three or more persons may assist in the beaming. The person or persons holding the warp are seated on the floor and take a firm grip on the warp. Bit by bit, one hand is placed behind the other. The warp must not slide between the hands, for it can easily become uneven.

The cord around the last link of the warp chain nearest the lease is now untied and the warp spread out at the reed. At this point the lease sticks are in front of the reed and it will be necessary to transpose the lease to a position in back of the reed (Fig. 14).

During beaming one person stands in front of the loom to move the beater and lease sticks forward and to see that no warp threads break. From time to time the warp should be checked to see that the tension is even across its entire width, and any unevenness may be regulated by giving additional pressure with the hands to the affected sections. Individual loose threads are gently drawn back toward the warp beam. This is done by the person who stands in front of the loom. The person holding the chain should not try to even the warp, and thus run the risk of entangling the strands.

The person who winds the warp also lays in the beam sticks and selvedge papers on the beam, as required. The selvedge papers are

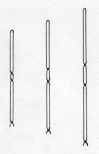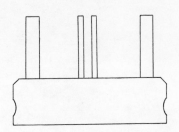

Fig. 16. Heddles. Fig. 17. Heddle block.

placed at either edge of the warp with the single thickness under the warp and the folded section just outside.

All warps are rolled on as tightly as possible; this is particularly important with linen warps.

In order to maintain an even tension when beaming a rug warp, it may be necessary to comb it at intervals. Such a method, however, can only be used on coarse, short warps.

When warping has been completed, the lease sticks are tied securely to the back beam or are hung so that during the threading process they are directly behind the harnesses. The end of the warp is then cut, and drawn out of the reed. The threads across the entire width are separated into groups which are tied with loop knots.

Beaming a warp with two leases and a raddle. This method of beaming differs from the above in that the raddle is not placed in the beater, but hangs independently (Fig. 15). When the warp has been transferred to the rod on the warp beam, the lease sticks are removed from the beaming lease. At the end of the warp the threading lease will appear and the lease sticks are then slipped into this lease before cutting. The upper bar of the raddle is taken off and the raddle removed.

Threading. A heddle consists of two loops and an eye (Fig. 16). The upper and lower heddle sticks are passed through the corresponding loops and the warp end is drawn through the eye. Heddles may be of varying sizes and qualities.

29

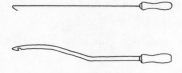

Fig. 19. Heddle hooks.   Fig. 18. Twisted heddles.

String heddles are generally used for handweaving. To make these heddles, cut string in suitable lengths and, using square knots (Fig. 28), tie over a heddle block (Fig. 17). The string should be held with the same tension and the knots tightly drawn, so that all of the heddles will be of equal length. When 50 to 100 heddles have been tied, they are removed from the block and twisted and tied together (Fig. 18).

Heddles for coarse warps are made of fish-net twine 12/12–12/9; for medium warps, of twine 12/6; and for fine warps, of twine 16/6–20/6.

The length of the heddles depends upon the harness number to be used in a weave. The larger the number, the longer the heddles which will be required to give a satisfactory shed. For any number up to an 8-harness weave, the heddles may measure 5 inches for each of the two loops, and the eye 1 inch. In multiple-harness weaves the loops may be 6 inches and the eye $\frac{3}{8}$ inch. In this case, a heddle hook is used to thread through the small eye of the heddle (Fig. 19).

30

Fig. 20. Threading
from the right.

In instances where two different sets of harnesses are used, as for *upphämta* weaves (Fig. 91), special heddles are used. For the set of pattern harnesses, heddles with 10 to 14 inches long loops and a small heddle eye often made of steel are used. Heddles with long eyes are used for the set of background harnesses, so that the pattern shed can remain open within the eyes of the background heddles. The loops are then 5 to 6 inches long, and the eye is 2 to 4 inches (Fig. 16 at right).

Steel heddles are also used in handweaving. These are set up in special frames. When ordering them, the closeness of the heddles per inch should be mentioned. They are to be recommended for very fine warps, since they cause less strain on the yarns than do string heddles.

The heddles have now been placed on the heddle sticks and counted. Each pair of sticks is examined carefully to see that the knots of the heddle eyes are all at the same height. Worn heddles are removed and any twisted heddles straightened out.

To prevent the heddles from sliding off the sticks, a cord may be tied across each stick. The heddle sticks are now placed in the harness holders (Fig. 20). To simplify checking, while threading, the warp ends are counted in groups in accordance with the draft (see page 52).

31

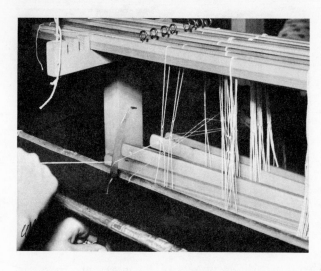

The threading may begin either at the right or the left. In handweaving, however, it is usually done from right to left (Fig. 20). The harness nearest the warp beam is considered the first harness. It greatly facilitates the task to have someone pass the threads to the person doing the threading. The threads are taken in due order at the lease, and unless otherwise stipulated, one thread is drawn through each heddle. When a group has been completed, the threading is checked and the group of threads tied with a loop knot.

Sleying. The reed is hung in front of the harness in a horizontal position below the heddle eyes. The warp should be accurately

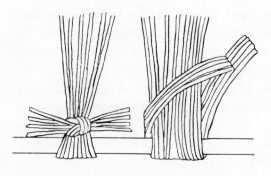

Fig. 22. Tying warp to the cloth beam rod.

centered on the reed and the first end sleyed in the outermost dent of its width. The warp ends are taken in proper order and are drawn through the dents with the aid of a reed hook. When a group of ends has been sleyed, it is checked, and again tied with a loop knot.

A warp of average closeness may be threaded with two ends in each dent; a more widely spaced warp, with one end; and a very close one, with three ends in a dent. Sleying may even be varied by threading a different number of ends in a dent or by leaving some dents empty to achieve a desired effect.

Sleying and threading may be a simultaneous operation when a *mechanical reed hook* is used (Fig. 21). This hook is constructed in such a way that it automatically travels along, one dent at a time, as it passes up and down in the reed. The upper part of the hook is bent so that it remains suspended in the reed while the warp ends are being threaded. When ordering a mechanical reed hook, the set of the reed as well as the direction of the sleying, from the right or the left, should be specified. When the warp is to be sleyed with two ends in each dent, two ends are first threaded. The hook is then pushed up into position and the threads laid in front of the hook, which draws them down through the reed. With practice, sleying with a mechanical hook will always be accurate. Another advantage is that there is less strain on the eyes than when using an ordinary reed hook.

Tying the warp to the cloth beam. The beater is hung in place on the loom and the reed centered in its groove. The knee beam and the breast beam are slipped into place. The rod which is connected to the cloth beam by means of a cord, is drawn forward over the knee beam and around the breast beam. A group of warp ends are first tied around the rod at its center, while another group of warp ends at each side is tied around the rod. A measurement is made to make certain that the rod is parallel to the breast beam.

Before continuing to tie the warp, a check is made to see that the warp passes without obstruction from the warp beam through

33

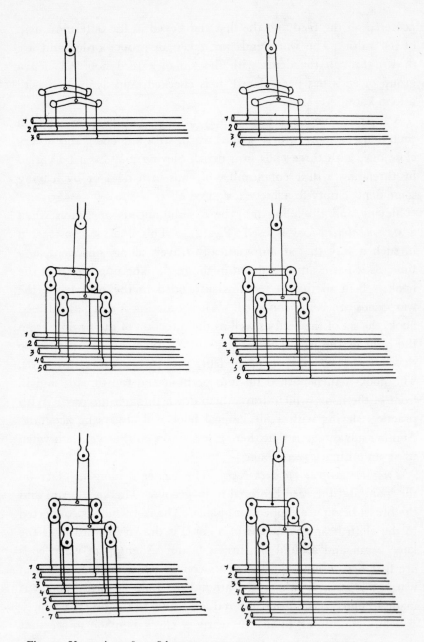

Fig. 23. Upper tie-up for 3–8 harnesses.

the lease and the heddles. The height of the harnesses is adjusted so that the warp is neither raised nor depressed.

To tie, take a group of threads (about as many as will measure one inch in the reed). Comb out the threads so that they are all equally taut and tie them around the rod, leaving as short ends as possible. One method is to divide the group of threads, drawing one-half over and one-half under the rod, and then tie them together with a knot which can easily be untied. Another method is to draw the whole group of threads over and under the rod, then divide them, and tie the ends together, as in Fig. 22.

Usually, it is necessary to adjust the knots again before the final firm knots are tied. If the first method has been used, a string is tied to one end of the rod and is threaded over the raised and under the lowered threads in order to make the entire warp level. The leveling string is drawn taut and tied to the other end of the rod. Then slide the hand over the surface of the warp to test the evenness of tension.

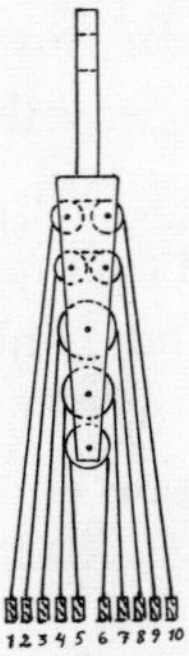

Fig. 24. *Dräll* pulleys.

Upper tie-up and treadle tie-up

After the warp has been tied on, the final process is the harness tie-up. In a counter-balanced loom the upper heddle sticks are tied to horses which operate over pulleys attached to the upper crossbar. The lower heddle sticks are tied to the treadles with or without the use of lamms. When the treadles are depressed, those harnesses which are tied to them will sink, and the other harnesses will rise in counter action. This will produce a good shed, if carefully balanced.

35

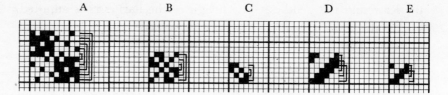

A   B   C   D   E

Fig. 25. Treadle tie-up draft; A 10-harness *dräll*, B 6-harness *dräll*, C half-*dräll*, D 6-harness Batavia and E 4-harness Batavia.

Upper tie-up. Horses and pulleys, or a combination of horses and pulleys, are required in the upper tie-up (Fig. 23). For a two-harness weave one pulley is used on each side (Fig. 13). For a three- or four-harness weave, two horses will be necessary on each side. These two horses are joined by a cord which is hung over a pulley (Fig. 23). When tying up from five to eight harnesses, the combined horse-pulley arrangement is used at each side, and is likewise hung over a pulley (Fig. 23).

So-called *dräll* pulleys may be used for a limited number of weaves. In this arrangement the pulleys are attached to a frame in such a way that the movement of one will not affect the others (Fig. 24). Thus, the two center harnesses are joined to each other by a cord running over the lowest pulley, the next two by the pulley above, and continuing in this manner until the two outermost harnesses are hung from the top pulley. The harnesses which are on the same cord rise and sink in counter action. An example of

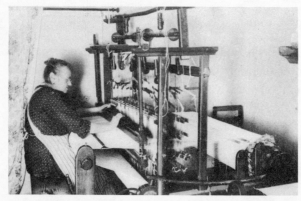

A weaver working on a multi-harness weave. Upper tie-up with horses and pulleys.

36

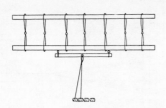

Fig. 26. Treadle tie-up without lamms.

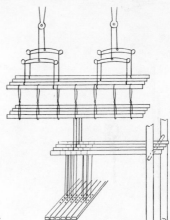

Fig. 27. Four-harness upper tie-up and treadle
tie-up for six treadles with lamms.

this counter action occurs in two-block *dräll* weaves, as may be
seen in the drafts in Fig. 25 A and B, as well as in drafts such as C.
Dräll pulleys are frequently used for 10-harness *dräll* weaves.

In drafts D and E there is also counter action, though not as in
the former instances, where the action takes place between the
outer harnesses and consecutively toward the inner harnesses.
Were *dräll* pulleys used in these latter drafts, a different arrangement
of the pulleys would have to be used.

Harness tie-up. To give proper support the horses and pulleys
should be placed above the harnesses, neither too far out on the
edge nor too near the center (Fig. 27). A cord is tied at the center
of one horse, drawn over the pulley and then tied to the center of
the other horse (Fig. 23). The horses are attached to the upper
heddle sticks, using loops of fish-net twine. The loops should be
placed correctly between the heddles. To determine this, measure
the distance from the center of the heddle stick to the point where
the inner end of the horse should be. The same distance is then
measured from the center of the reed. The warp and heddles at
this point are drawn slightly to one side, an end of the twine is
looped around the stick and the other end slipped over the horse

37

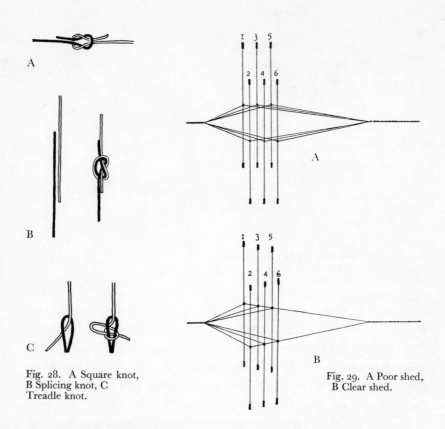

Fig. 28. A Square knot,
B Splicing knot, C
Treadle knot.

Fig. 29. A Poor shed,
B Clear shed.

with a hitch knot. Next, measure the size of the horse and compare this measurement in the reed. At this point, attach the twine loops to the outer end of the heddle stick and the outer end of the horse. The combined harness-pulley (Fig. 23) is attached in similar manner, though with cords instead of twine loops.

The height of the harnesses is determined to a certain extent by the type of the weave. For a reversible weave, the harnesses are tied in the *center position*, that is, with the warp passing through the center of the heddle eye. In a warp-faced weave the harnesses should be tied *higher*; and in a weft-faced weave, *lower*.

Lower tie-up. When a loom has no lamms, a short stick is attached to the lower heddle stick (Fig. 26). A cord from the center of this short stick is tied directly to the treadle. However, if more than two harnesses and treadles are used, the cords are likely to pull off center and produce a poor shed. To counteract this, some weavers draw all of the cords through a ring and tie the treadles from this central point. It is also a good idea to tie a cord around the lower heddle sticks and make a loop knot through each of the outer heddles to prevent their sliding off the sticks.

Present-day looms are equipped with *lamms*, which operate between the harnesses and treadles so that the cords pull straight down from the lamms to the treadles (Fig. 27). The lamms are mounted on an axle attached to one side of the loom. There should always be as many lamms as there are harnesses.

Tie-up of lamms. Find the center of the warp in the reed, and at this point separate the heddles slightly on the lower heddle sticks. Tie a cord at the middle of each of these heddle sticks. In each lamm locate the hole which is in the center of the loom and tie a loop of cord through it. The first harness is then tied to the first lamm, the second harness to the second lamm, and so on, using the so-called treadle knot (Fig. 28). The lamms are tied in horizontal position. In place of loops and cords, chains hooked into screw eyes may be used (see p. 242 and Fig. 133).

Treadle tie-up. The lamms contain rows of holes on either side of the loops. Cords are put through these holes and are then tied to the treadles. The spaces between the holes on the lamms should be equal to the width of the treadles. Tie up the treadles from the back of the loom. Accordingly, the tie-up draft should be read in reverse. For every black square in the tie-up draft, thread a cord in the corresponding hole in the lamm (see draft in Fig. 38). Attach looped cords to the treadles and tie the lamm cords through these loops, using the "treadle knot." It is not advisable to tie more than two cords to the same loop. The height of the treadles should be adjusted so that when depressed they almost touch the floor.

The *treadle knot* (Fig. 28 C) is made in the following manner: Run the cord from the lamm through the loop on the treadle and hold it with the left hand. Now, with the right hand slip a loop

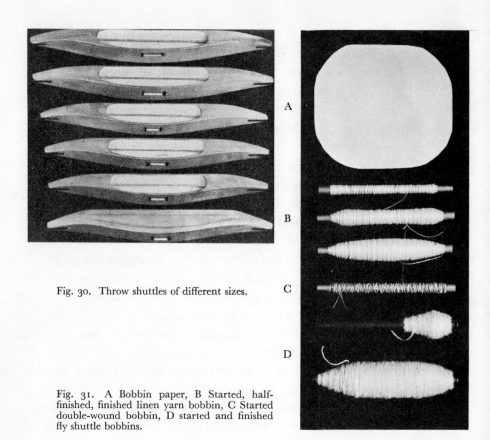

Fig. 30. Throw shuttles of different sizes.

A

B

C

D

Fig. 31. A Bobbin paper, B Started, half-finished, finished linen yarn bobbin, C Started double-wound bobbin, D started and finished fly shuttle bobbins.

around and *below* the treadle loop and pull tightly. The treadle knot is always used when tying a cord to a loop.

In this connection it should be noted that all knots used in weaving should be as simple and effective as possible; should be properly tightened and leave no long trailing ends. To prevent the knots from slipping down into the holes of the lamms and treadles, washers of suitable size threaded on the cords are recommended. Fig. 28 shows, in addition to the treadle knot, a square knot (A) and a knot (B) used in place of the weaver's knot (Fig. 2), for tying a very smooth yarn, such as rayon or worsted.

40

For multi-harness weaves it is difficult to get a clear shed if all the cords are tied to the treadles with equal tension. The warp threads in the heddles on the harnesses toward the back must be lowered and raised more than those on the forward harnesses, in order to have the entire warp at the same level in the shed. Thus, it is obvious that the cords from the back harnesses should be very taut, while there should be successively less tension as the cords are tied toward the front, enabling these latter to rise and sink to a lesser extent (Fig. 29 B). Since there may be considerable difference in tension, some weavers may prefer to tie all of the cords equally taut, and instead, raise the beater so that the lower part of it touches the warp, and levels the lower shed.

Preparation of the weft

The preparation of the weft is very much simpler than that of the warp. In most cases all that is required is to *wind bobbins* or, if heavy yarn is used, to *wind* on *stick shuttles*. For laid-in weaves, so-called *butterfly bobbins* are made.

Bobbin-winding. The weft is wound on paper or wooden quills with the aid of a bobbin winder. The type of bobbin is determined by the *shuttle* to be used. The *throw shuttle* is used for ordinary handweaving (Fig. 30).

It is extremely important to select a shuttle of the right size and construction. An ordinary shuttle is about 12 inches long, $\frac{3}{4}$ inch high, with a bobbin chamber $4\frac{3}{4}$ inches in length. Larger shuttles are, of course, used for heavy yarns, and smaller ones for very fine qualities. The underside of the shuttle is constructed in such a way that it will glide over the warp easily with the least amount of friction. The bobbin spindle should not be too long, as that will strain the spring, which may easily break, as well as cause the spindle itself to bend out of shape. On one side of the shuttle is an aperture through which the weft yarn is threaded.

41

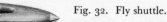
Fig. 32. Fly shuttle.

Paper bobbins have the advantage of being usable in low shuttles. Wooden quills, which have flanges at the ends, require higher shuttles than those described above. The paper for the bobbins is cut to fit the size of the bobbin chamber and the corners rounded as shown in Fig. 31 A.

The bobbin paper is twisted tightly around the spindle of the bobbin winder. Before the paper bobbin has been completely wound around the spindle, the weft yarn is attached and is wound back and forth on the bobbin (Fig. 31 B). This process should be carried out evenly across the bobbin with a slight swelling at each end. As the bobbin nears completion, the yarn should be brought gradually toward the center. A bobbin of cotton or woolen yarn may have a steeper incline at each end than would be advisable for a linen bobbin. In winding a bobbin using linen yarn the thread should be held very tightly.

If the bobbins are to be double-wound, i.e., with two strands of yarn, each yarn should first be wound on a larger spool. Then proceed to wind the bobbin rapidly back and forth, being careful to see that both strands have the same tension. When yarns of different kinds are being wound together, the less elastic yarns may be slowed down by attaching weights to these spools.

A *fly shuttle* (Fig. 32) is another type of shuttle. It has straight sides and metal-tipped ends. The base is often slanted, thereby aiding the shuttle in remaining on its path as it passes through the open shed. The bobbin is attached at one end of the shuttle chamber

A

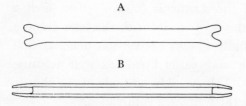

B

Fig. 33. Stick shuttles A and B.

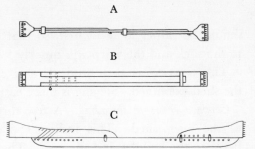

Fig. 34. Stretchers, A Steel stretcher with extension, B wooden stretcher, C wooden stretcher with reinforcement.

with the aperture for the yarn at the other. There should be several holes at this end of the shuttle in order to control the bobbin release. In winding the yarn on cardboard or wooden quills, commence at one end and continue successively toward the other end (Fig. 31 D).

Stick shuttles may be of very simple construction, as in Fig. 33 A, or of somewhat more elaborate design, as in B. Yarn or rags are wound on these shuttles.

Hand bobbins, also called butterfly bobbins, are made by winding yarn between the thumb and little finger of the left hand and crossing the yarn over the palm of the hand. The beginning end of yarn is left hanging, so that it may be easily located, while the other end is wound around the center of the cross and fastened with a half-hitch.

Check of loom set-up

First of all, the loom must be *level* and the beater correctly hung. With the beater hanging straight down, measure the distance from the beater to the breast beam at each side. If necessary, adjustments are then made so that the beater will strike evenly. The beater is hung at the correct height when the warp is in the middle of the reed.

Now check the threading by shuttling in a few shots of the same yarn as is to be used in the weft, or use a different *colored yarn,* so that the weave will show up more clearly. The tension of the warp

43

should be rather loose at first, so that the first shots will beat up to the stick and the warp will quickly "weave into position."

The weaving is then studied, and each treadle depressed and the shed examined. Sleying is more easily checked in a tabby shed.

Common errors in threading. A few threads remain in the middle of the open shed. This indicates that the threads are crossed between the heddles and the reed. These threads should be drawn out and sleyed correctly in the reed.

Loose threads on the right or wrong side indicate that they have not been threaded through the heddles. They must be drawn out and threaded through the heddle eyes.

Errors in the weave across the entire width of the material show that the harnesses have not been correctly *tied* to the treadles. One treadle at a time is therefore depressed and the movement of the harnesses compared with the tie-up draft, so that the error may be corrected.

A *locked shed* may be due to one of the following causes: the lease sticks are too close to the heddles, the heddle sticks are tied together, the lamms are caught up, or the treadle cords crossed.

Certain warp threads bind incorrectly, which is caused by faulty threading. If the threads have been counted and the number agrees with the number of heddles, the error is a local one and the incorrectly threaded strands should be drawn out and rethreaded. But if an occasional thread has been drawn through on the wrong harness, the heddle may be untied and then retied on the correct harness. If the error proves to be of greater extent than purely local, all of the threads to the nearest selvedge must be redone.

The weave shows close or open stripes in the direction of the warp which do not form part of the pattern. This is caused by incorrect sleying. The threads must be drawn out of the reed and correctly sleyed to the nearest selvedge.

The *weft "jumps"* at intervals in the weave, because the tie-up is uneven. Adjust the cords of the upper tie-up as well as the treadle cords.

A common error in the upper tie-up is when the cords connecting

44

the horses to the harnesses are not properly *placed* on the heddle sticks or between the heddles. Another difficulty occurs when the cord which connects the lower heddle stick to the lamm or treadle is not in the center of the stick between the two middle heddles. Or perhaps one of the harnesses is higher than the others. In this instance the cord from the harness to the treadle should be tightened. During these adjustments the harnesses should rest on the harness holders, or the harnesses kept level by other means.

Weaving. Weaving may be divided into three movements: *throwing the shuttle, beating* and *treadling*.

The shuttle is held in one hand, is *thrown through the open shed*, and is received at the opposite side by the other hand, which at the same time holds back the beater. The shuttle should be thrown in and drawn out of the shed with precision so that the selvedge will be even. Beginners often hold the thumb on the bobbin and thus stretch the weft, in an effort to avoid loops at the selvedge. This causes the weave to "draw in" and threads soon break. Therefore, it is much better at first not to think too much about the selvedges, and instead strive for an *even rhythm* in shuttling.

When *beating*, hold the hand at the center of the beater, and press against the weave while treadling. In ordinary weaving, one stroke of the beater is sufficient, if effectively done. But when wide and closely set materials are woven, such as damask cloths, an additional beat is made after treadling. The "after-beat" also assists in clearing the shed in a multiple-harness weave.

In *treadling*, the treadle should not be depressed more than is necessary to open the shed sufficiently to permit the passage of the shuttle. The weight of the weaver's body should rest on the loom bench and not on the treadles. *One should at all times remember to avoid any unnecessary strain upon the warp.*

Beating is usually done in an *"open shed,"* as described above. However, in certain types of weaves, such as weft-faced rep and others where the weft covers the warp, the beat is made after treadling. This is called beating in a *closed shed*. In this instance, the weft is shuttled in, and is drawn up in an arc by the shuttle, where-upon the next treadle is depressed and the weft beaten up. In weaving wide rugs, a single arc of the weft is not sufficient; instead, small even arcs are formed across the entire width. Weft-faced rep may easily become ribbed at the selvedges. This is due to beating in a closed shed, and may be avoided if the last weft is stretched somewhat at the selvedge before the next weft is shuttled in. This weft is then held firmly at the selvedge while the remainder of the weft is drawn up in an arc.

As the weaving builds up closer to the beater, *more warp is rolled forward* and the lease sticks moved back. The lease sticks should not be tied to the back beam.

Avoid too great a *tension* of the *warp*, the one exception being that of a rug warp. Linen fabrics will acquire a sheen and be more beautiful, and woolens are softer, if the warp is not too tightly stretched. In addition, it is easier to treadle, to beat and to hold out the selvedges, if the tension is not too firm.

Stretchers or *temples* are used to hold out the selvedges. These are constructed either of steel or of wood (Fig. 34). An extension may be added to the steel stretcher for wide weaves, as seen in A. For very heavy or especially wide weaves the wooden stretcher, B, is used. One with a particularly strong reinforcement is shown in C. To adjust the stretcher to the proper length, place it against the reed, bottom side up, i.e., with the barbs upward. The outer selvedge threads should reach to the half-way point of the barbs, which must be fine and straight. The stretcher barbs are then fitted into both edges of the weave about one-half inch down from the edge of the weaving. If the stretcher is fastened into the material too far out, or too far in, there is danger of damaging the selvedge. It may at times even be necessary to loosen the tension of the warp when inserting the stretcher. The stretcher should be moved so frequently that it will progress gradually along the entire selvedge. In some instances, a stretcher can be dispensed with, as in weaving narrow linens, narrow art weaves, or rugs.

46

At intervals during weaving, check to see that no *warp threads have broken*. When repairing a warp thread, first locate the thread in the shed and then separate the other threads on either side, back to the heddles. The empty heddle is then easily found and can be rethreaded, as well as the empty dent in the reed. If a broken thread is observed at once, the two ends may be twisted around each other and laid in opposite directions in the weft under a few warp threads in the open shed. This can only be done when the yarn in the warp and the weft is the same. If a section of warp thread is missing in the woven material, it may be repaired later by being threaded in between the wefts in accordance with the pattern. If the warp is so coarse that no knots can pass through the reed, the broken thread should be repaired using a long thread reaching to the lease. Then, instead of cutting off the other thread, continue to weave about a half yard and draw forward the original thread. In this way the knot never passes through the reed.

In *splicing weft yarn*, lay the end of the new thread a half-inch or so over the other weft thread in the open shed. Knots should be avoided whenever possible in a weave.

Checking the degree of closeness in the weft. A handweaver should be able to gauge the closeness of a weave by sight. In a tabby weave, for example, one can see that two warp threads and two weft threads form a square. In a twill weave, the set of the warp and the weft is equal when the twill diagonal is at a $45°$ angle to the weft.

Another way to judge the closeness of the weft is to measure as follows: lay in a short piece of colored thread in the shed. Shuttle in as many shots of the weft as will measure one-half inch, lay in colored thread again, shuttle in the same number of shots and continue in this way until two inches have been woven. The closeness of the weft is correct if the colored thread is placed at exactly one-half inch intervals.

When weaving a fabric in horizontal stripes or in checks, the intervals may be marked off on a paper strip. If a material is woven in two lengths which will later be sewn together, a cloth strip may accompany the first length and the intervals marked on it. This strip should then follow the second length as a guide.

To measure the number of yards woven, consideration should be given to the fact that thirty-six inches of "raw" length is equivalent to about $36\frac{3}{4}$ inches on the loom, or even more, depending on the elasticity of the fabric.

The warp and the stretcher do not need to be loosened overnight, though this is advisable if weaving is interrupted for several days. In the case of wide rug looms, however, there is a danger of the beams becoming bent, and for this reason, it is well to release the tension of the warp at the close of a working day.

The end of the warp may be woven to within approximately twelve inches, when using four harnesses, and somewhat less may be woven when there are more harnesses. When the woven material is ready to be *removed from the loom*, the harness holders are placed under the upper heddle sticks, the lease sticks are withdrawn and the warp thrums cut off. The cloth-beam ratchet is then released, and as the cloth is unrolled from the beam, it is laid in folds over the breast beam. The cloth is now ready to be examined and mended, measured, weighed and rolled.

WEAVE CONSTRUCTION AND ART WEAVES

INTRODUCTION

An ordinary weave or fabric consists of two thread systems at right angles to one another. One thread system is called the *warp* and the other the *weft* (Fig. 36).

As described in the preceding chapter, the warp is set up in the loom so that the harnesses cause some threads to be lowered while others are raised, and thus a *shed* is formed. A shot of weft is shuttled through and beaten, after which a new shed is opened; a new weft shot is made, and another shed opened. In this way the weave grows.

The system according to which the warp and weft are interwoven is called the *weave construction*. To draft the weave construction in a clear and simple way, squared paper is used (Fig. 35). The vertical squares in the diagram or draft represent the warp threads, and the horizontal squares represent the weft threads.

A *repeat* is marked off in the lower left-hand corner of every draft, and according to this the warp and weft are repeated (Figs. 35

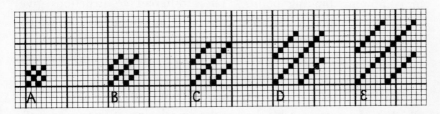

Fig. 35. Examples of drafts.

49

and 36). Within a repeat every warp thread must be interlaced with the weft at least once, i.e., lowered at least once for one or more wefts and raised for the others. Such a simple weave construction within repeats of different sizes is shown in Fig. 35 A–E. The first thread is lowered for the first weft, the second thread for the second weft, the third thread for the third weft, etc. (Figs. 36 and 37). Thus, a filled-in square in the draft signifies that the warp thread is lowered and that the weft lies over the warp thread on the right side.

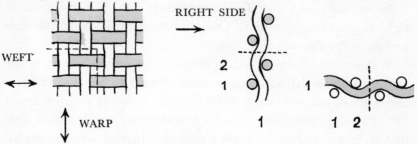

Fig. 36. Diagram of tabby weave Fig. 35 A. Diagram at right: cross section of weft on first warp thread and of warp on first weft thread.

Should the size of the repeat continue to be enlarged and each warp thread interlaced with the weft only once, the floats of warp and weft threads would be too long and would produce a textile structurally weak. On the other hand, many different weaves may be obtained if there are several different binding points on each warp thread, or if the construction is modified by doubling, staggering or combining binding points. These different constructions give the fabrics sufficient durability, as well as characteristics which make them suitable for varied purposes.

There are three classifications of weaves which are the basis of all others and are thus called the *basic weaves*.

The first classification comprises one type only, the *tabby weave*, which is characterized by the regular interlacing of warp and weft threads (Fig. 36).

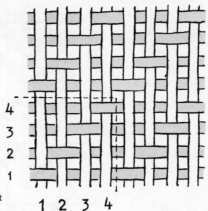

4
3
2
1

Fig. 37. Diagram of twill weave, draft
Fig. 35 C.

1 2 3 4

The second classification consists of the *twill weaves*, in which the binding points are staggered and produce diagonal lines on the fabric (Fig. 37).

The third classification includes the *satin weaves*, in which the binding points are spaced and give satin fabrics a smooth surface.

The *derivative weaves* are obtained from the basic weaves when warp or weft threads are doubled, transposed or combined in such a way that weaves with completely different characteristics appear.

Then there is a group of weaves in which the *basic* or *derivative* weaves are *incorporated* to a greater or lesser extent. In this study of weave construction, they have been included in the various sections where similarity of construction has been the deciding factor.

Art weaves are usually classified as a separate group. In these weaves the construction is of secondary importance, the chief consideration being the pattern which is produced either by color effects, interlocking or knotting of the weft. The most common art weaves are rosepath, monk's belt, *upphämta*, the inlay techniques of *rölakan* and *krabbasnår*, *dukagång*, the figured double-weave called *finnväv* (or Bohus-weave in Sweden), and pile weaves, such as *rya* and *flossa*. However, since no clear-cut division can be drawn between art weaves and other weaves, those which are shuttled like rosepath, monk's belt, *upphämta* and double-weave, have been

51

Treadling draft.

Pattern diagram.

Treadle tie-up plan.

Threading draft.

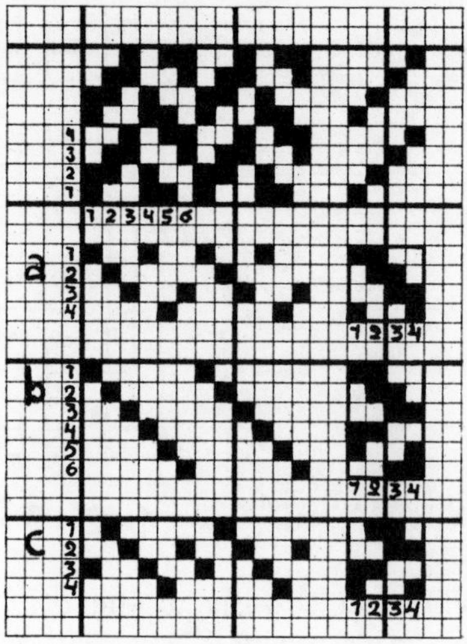

Fig. 38.

placed in their respective classifications among the above-mentioned weaves. Weaves which are interlocked, such as *rölakan* and *krabbasnår* have been treated as one group, while the knotted weaves have been classified as "pile weaves."

To use a pattern diagram in a practical way when setting up a loom, it is provided with a threading draft, a treadle tie-up draft and a treadling draft (Fig. 38).

The *threading draft* indicates how many harnesses are required in the weave, as well as the order of threading. The weave requires as many harnesses as there are different interlaced or bound warp threads within the repeat. All threads lowered or raised in the same weft, whichever the case may be, bind similarly and are therefore threaded on the same harness.

Fig. 38 shows a pattern diagram with six warp threads in the repeat, of which the first, second, third and fifth threads bind differently, the fourth binding like the first, and the sixth like the third. The threading, therefore, comprises four harnesses with those threads which bind similarly on the same harnesses. In Fig. 39 four harnesses are also required, while the repeat includes eight

Fig. 39.

threads of which the first four are completely different and the last four are similar to the first four, although in reversed order.

A draft should be made as simple as possible, so that it can be carried out quickly and with the least possibility of error. The simplest draft is the one in consecutive order. This means that all the threads in the repeat are threaded in direct sequence (first, second, third, fourth, etc.) on their respective harnesses, and all the wefts are shuttled in, depressing the treadles, one following the other in the same manner. From the point of view of simplicity, the first threading in Fig. 36 *a* is not satisfactory and may be described as in *jumping* order. However, if the threading is done in consecutive order, as in *b*, six harnesses would be required, which is certainly more difficult to weave with than four. Threading *c* indicates that while retaining four harnesses, the order may be changed and thus become more nearly continuous. This would, consequently, be the best threading for the pattern in question. There are other reasons, as well, for altering the first threading, which will be discussed in connection with drafts to be taken up later.

Drafts (threading and treadling) have various names according to their order of construction. The most common are: consecutive or straight (Fig. 38 *b*), pointed or reversed (Fig. 55), broken (Fig.

53

52), jumping (Fig. 38 *a*), advancing, condensed and extended (Fig. 72), and in various groups (Fig. 97 A).

The *treadle tie-up plan* indicates how the harnesses are to be tied to the treadles. A shaded square in the plan represents the cord that connects the harness with the treadle.

The weave requires as many treadles as there are different wefts within the repeat. For all wefts binding similarly, the same treadle is depressed. To ascertain which harnesses are to be tied to the different treadles, each weft is examined to see what warp threads are covered by the weft. In Fig. 38, the first, fourth and fifth threads are under the first weft. They are threaded on the first and fourth harnesses of the threading draft and in the tie-up plan there are two shaded squares for the first treadle representing these two harnesses (draft *a*). In the second weft, the first, second and fourth warp threads are lowered. These are threaded on the first and second harnesses and the two corresponding squares are shaded for the second treadle. For the third weft, the second, third and sixth threads are lowered. They are threaded on the second and third harnesses and the tie-up marked for the third treadle. Finally, the third, fifth and sixth threads are lowered for the fourth weft. They are threaded on the third and fourth harnesses and the tie-up indicated for the fourth treadle. The other drafts are carried out in the same way.

The treadling draft specifies the order in which the treadles are depressed for the different wefts. In the above example, each weft within the repeat is different and, therefore, the treadling follows in consecutive order. In Fig. 39, the first four wefts are different and the treadling begins in consecutive order. Thereafter, the fifth weft is like the third, and the treadling draft shows that the third treadle should be used for this weft. Likewise, the sixth weft resembles the second; the seventh weft, the first; and the eighth weft, the fourth.

Following these principles, drafts may be made for all weave constructions. A suggestion is offered to work out some of the

54

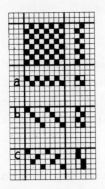

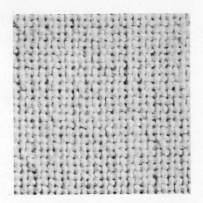

Fig. 40. Tabby drafts.   Tabby weave.

drafts in this book. Using squared paper, cover up the treadling and tie-up drafts on the following weaves and work out the drafts yourself: Figs. 55 L and Q, 57 A, 59 A, 66 A, 67 C. Then compare your results with the original ones.

Dish towel in tabby weave. Warp and weft, yarn in natural linen No. 20; stripes colored cotton 16/2. Reed: 18 or 19 dents per inch with 2 ends in each dent.

55

TABBY WEAVE AND ITS DERIVATIVES

Tabby weave (plain weave)

This weave has a repeat which comprises two warp threads, and two wefts only (Fig. 40). The first thread is lowered for the first weft and raised for the second. The second thread is raised for the first weft and lowered for the second. Warp and weft threads continually interlace and never cover more than one weft or one warp thread without binding (cf. Fig. 36).

The draft may, of course, be written with two harnesses and two treadles. It is more usual, however, for closely set warps to be threaded on four harnesses to avoid crowding the heddles on the frames and thus obstruct the action of the sheds. Either threading draft *b* or *c* may be used for four harnesses. The advantage of the latter is that the two harnesses which are lowered at the same time are next to each other and are hung together. This results in a more even shed.

A fabric in tabby weave has a flat, unpatterned surface, which is reversible and has a duller finish than a weave using the very same yarns, but with longer floats. Due to its firm weave, the tabby technique is widely used. With a minimum of yarn it is a pliable and durable fabric.

Rep and basket weaves are derived from the tabby weave by doubling warp and weft threads. Thus, warp-faced rep is obtained by doubling the wefts while the warp threads are single. In weft-faced rep the warp threads are doubled and the weft is single. Basket weave is obtained by doubling both warp and weft equally.

Warp-faced rep

The draft for a 2/2 warp-faced rep may be seen in Fig. 41 A, and for a 3/1 warp-faced rep in B. The numbers indicate that the wefts in A are double and in B are alternating triple and single. An example of greater variation in wefts is shown in C.

RIGHT
→

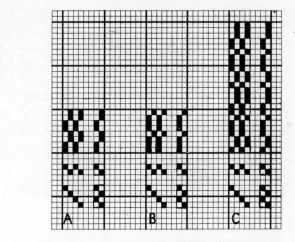

Cross section of wefts for the first
and second threads in A.

Fig. 41. Warp-faced rep drafts.

1 2

In this type of fabric the warp creates the main effect and should be set so closely that the weft is completely covered. As the warp curves over and under the wefts, which lie fairly straight, an effect of horizontal lines in the cloth appears. For this reason, warp-faced rep is often called horizontal rep. The ribs are further emphasized when alternate dark and light warp threads are used.

A warp-faced rep fabric, in contrast to most weaves, is more elastic warp-wise. For this reason a higher percentage of "take-up" of warp must be considered when calculating the amount required (see yarn calculation).

The warp may be threaded on two harnesses, but because of the close set, it is preferable to thread in consecutive order on four harnesses or according to Fig. 40 C. The double wefts may be

2
1

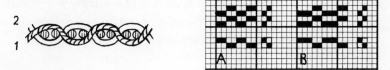

Cross section of threads for first and
second weft in A.

Fig. 42. Weft-faced rep drafts.

57

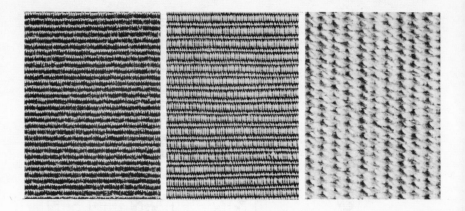

Weaves with warp-faced rep according to Fig. 41 A and B, and weave with weft-faced rep according to Fig. 42 A.

woven in various ways. If the weft shots are to lie in parallel ribs, they may be shuttled in with *two* shuttles and with one beat between each. Or *one* shuttle may be used, but it must then be passed around the outer selvedge to prevent the weft from slipping back when shuttling in the second shot. In an automatic loom, additional selvedge binding is added to catch the weft. The weft yarn may also be double-wound or may be replaced by a yarn that is twice as coarse as the warp.

Warp-faced rep is used for curtains, rugs, etc., as well as for machine-woven rep fabrics of cotton, silk and worsted.

Weft-faced rep

The draft for a 2/2 weft-faced rep is shown in Fig. 42 A, and another for a 3/2 weft-faced rep in B. The numbers 2/2 indicate that the weft passes over two and under two warp threads, and numbers 3/2 that the weft passes over three and under two warp threads alternately.

In this weave then, it is the weft which gives character to the fabric, and the warp should be spaced to such an extent that the

Rug in weft-faced rep with *tvist* stripes.

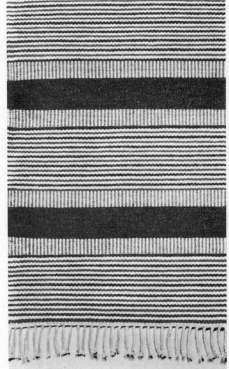

Detail of rug in weft-faced rep with *tvist* stripes. Warp: natural linen 6/4. Weft: coarse wool and cow hair yarn. Reed: 5 ends per inch, one end in each dent.

59

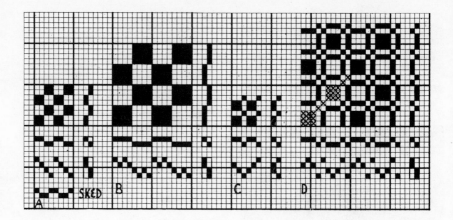

Fig. 43. Basket weave drafts.

weft will cover it. This gives an effect of vertical ridges. If alternating light and dark yarns are used in the weft, the ribbing becomes
more distinct (called *tvist* in Swedish). The weft is often laid in
an arc, before beating, and this will aid in covering the warp. In
this case the additional amount of yarn required should be taken
into consideration in the yarn estimate.

Warp-faced reps are threaded on two harnesses, either with two
similarly woven threads in one heddle, or each in adjacent heddles
on the same harness. In the latter case, they will lie parallel in

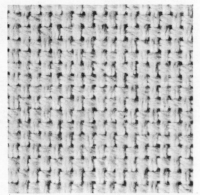

Basket weave according to Fig. 43A.

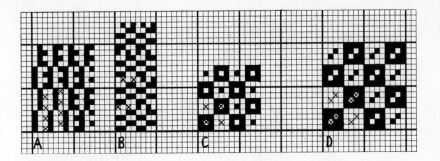

Fig. 44. Rep and basket weave drafts with binding threads.

the weave. A heavier warp thread than the weft may be substituted for the two warp threads.

Weft-faced reps are frequently used in handweaving, either as plain weaves or as backgrounds for art weaves.

Basket weave

Fig. 43 A shows a 2/2 basket weave and B, one in 4/4. In the former, both warp and weft are double, while in the latter they are quadrupled. The set of warp and weft should be equal, so that, as in tabby, both are equally emphasized.

Threading is usually done on four harnesses and the warp threads will then lie parallel in the weave. For similar wefts the same rules apply as for warp-faced rep. C and D show pattern drafts of variations of basket weave. Fig. D has been drafted showing the variation diagonally in the repeat, as for example: $\frac{1\ 3\ 1}{3\ 1\ 1}$ in the ✕-filled squares. The second threading draft on four harnesses is preferable to the first on two harnesses. Two treadles, however, are all that are necessary.

Basket weaves are used for suitings and as backgrounds for patterned linen weaves.

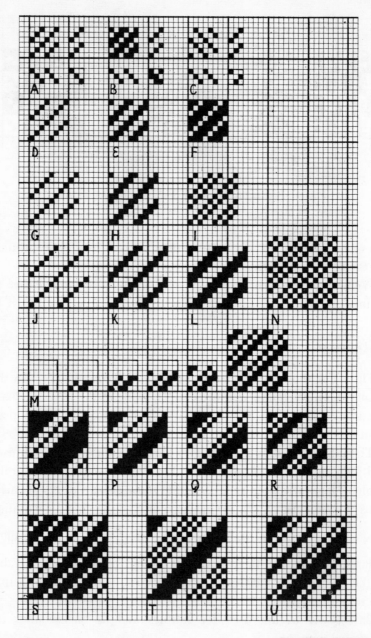

Fig. 45. Twill drafts.

Suiting in 4-harness Batavia twill. Warp-spun and weft-spun wool. Reeds: 12–13 dents per inch, 2 ends in a dent, 10 warp threads and 9 wefts per ⅜ inch.

Rep and basket weaves with extra binding threads

Binding threads are used partly to keep similar warp and weft threads apart, and partly to obtain a firmer weave.

Fig. 44 A shows a 4/4 warp-faced rep with a tabby warp thread following two rep threads. The repeat, therefore, includes six warp threads and eight weft threads. The tabby creates the effect of wider and flatter ribs, and prevents the warp from sliding along the weft.

A thin cotton yarn is used as the binding warp and should be completely concealed by the rep threads. Bouclé yarns and the like are often used in rep fabrics, which give them a somewhat firmer weave.

Basket weaves may also have binding threads, if a firmer fabric is desired.

In drafting, two harnesses are needed for the rep threads and two for the tabby threads, as: 1, 2, 3, 1, 2, 4. If six harnesses are available, this would be a better draft: 1, 2, 3, 4, 5, 6. Four treadles are required, treadled as follows: 1, 2, 1, 2, 3, 4, 3, 4.

Fig. 44 B shows a 2/2 weft-faced rep with one tabby binding weft thread following four rep wefts. The binding wefts prevent the rep wefts from sliding along the warp. The draft for this pattern

63

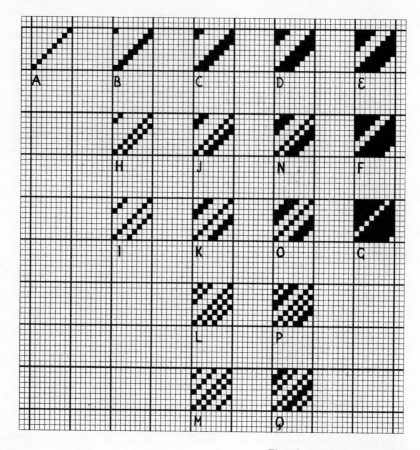

Fig. 46. Eight-harness twills.

would be threaded on four harnesses, as follows: 1, 2, 3, 4 and treadled 1, 2, 1, 2, 3, 1, 2, 1, 2, 4.

Fig. 44 C and D show basket weaves where a firmer fabric is obtained by moving the center point or points from the weft square to the warp square. Four harnesses and four treadles should be used for C, and six harnesses and treadles for D.

64

TWILL WEAVES AND THEIR DERIVATIVES

Twill weaves

These weaves are characterized by the movement of the binding points, one thread to the side in each weft shot, making diagonal lines in the weave. The slant is usually to the right, the weave then being called the right-hand twill (Fig. 45 A). When the diagonal is to the left, it is called the left-hand twill (Fig. 45 C). Right-hand twill is always used for suiting, the diagonals in that direction indicating the right side of the material.

Twill weaves may be produced from repeats of a variety of sizes, from 3 × 3 and upwards. In the basic twills the number of threads in the repeat and the number of harnesses and treadles required are always the same. Consequently, the size of the repeat often indicates the number of harnesses necessary. Thus, three-harness twills may be seen in Fig. 45 A, B, C; four-harness twills in D, E, F; five-harness twills in G, H, I, etc.

In drafting basic twills, the threading and treadling are always in consecutive order. For example, in Fig. 45 A, B, C, the threading draft would read 1, 2, 3 and treadling 1, 2, 3. A draft of a pattern

Suiting in twill, Fig. 46 N. Curtain material as in O.

in consecutive order has a tie-up plan which is like the figure in the repeat, but the diagonal goes in the opposite direction. In other words, in a right-hand twill, the tie-up plan slants to the left. Similarly, a twelve-harness twill, like Fig. 45 O, is threaded and treadled in consecutive order: 1, 2, 3, 4, 5, 6, 7, 8, 9, 10, 11, 12. The tie-up plan will be like the repeat, but slanting diagonally to the left.

Fig. 45 M illustrates the method of working out a twill weave step by step. To the right the weave is drawn in four repeats to give a clearer idea of what it looks like.

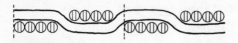

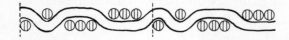

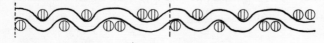

Fig. 47. Cross section of warp threads in first weft in drafts D, N and P.

1. Select one complete repeat, which in this instance has six warp threads and six wefts, thus making a six-harness twill. Enclose the repeat on the graph paper with a heavy line.

2. Observe the pattern on six warp threads. M shows one lowered warp thread and one raised, two lowered and two raised, in this way: $\dfrac{1\ 2}{1\ 2}$.

3. Start filling in the squares of the first weft, beginning at the bottom of the repeat. Shaded squares represent lowered warp threads and empty squares raised warp threads. Thus, from left to right for the first weft, fill in the first square, leave the second empty, fill in squares three and four, and leave five and six empty.

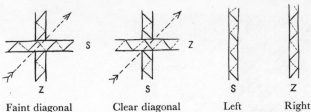

Fig. 48.   Faint diagonal   Clear diagonal   Left   Right

4. Wefts two and three follow the same procedure, but each time the diagonals are moved one thread to the right. Coming to weft number four, remember to stay within the limited repeat. Instead of shading a square on the seventh warp thread, fill in the square on the first warp thread in the repeat. Wefts five and six are drafted similarly. Observe that there are the same number of shaded squares or binding points on every weft thread in the repeat. There are, in this pattern, three shaded squares on each warp thread of the repeat.

Twill drafts requiring a larger number of harnesses are shown in Fig. 45 O–U. These repeats are clear patterns; otherwise multiple harnesses would not be justified.

It is evident that as the number of possible variations of a weave increases, there are more harnesses. To ascertain all the different twill variations which can be produced, a table may be worked out. The following is a table for eight-harness twills:

A twill weave may be *non-reversible* or *reversible*. A non-reversible

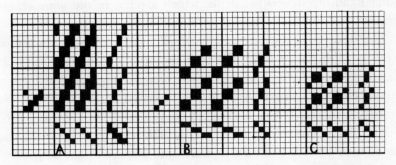

Fig. 49. Enlarged twill.

Fabric using draft Fig. 49 C.

twill has either a predominantly warp effect or a weft effect on the face side, or the warp and weft effects may be equal, but the pattern different on the face and reverse sides. Of the eight-harness twills shown, A is a clear warp-face twill, while B and C, as well as the drafts shown below these, are predominantly warp-face. E and F are chiefly weft-face, while B and C are similar, though as warp-face twills. G is a clear weft-face twill, and O an example of a twill with equal warp and weft effects, but with dissimilar patterns on the face and reverse sides.

Among the reversible twills are those which have half the threads in the repeat lowered in turn, and the other half raised. These are known as Batavia twills. D is a Batavia twill. N, P, and Q, on the other hand, are reversible twills, which are not in the same classification. Of the drafts in Fig. 45, E and L are Batavia twills.

The distance a warp thread is raised over a certain number of wefts is called a *warp float*. The term *weft float* is used when the weft lies over a certain number of warp threads. Fig. 47 illustrates a cross-section of warp threads in the first weft in the drafts D, N, and P. Of these, D has the longest floats, and P the shortest.

The floats also affect the *set* of the fabric, in other words, the number of threads per inch in warp and weft (cf. page 224, computation of set). Using the same yarn, a fabric woven according

68

to draft D would be a closer and thicker weave than one woven according to draft P, which would have a thinner, but firmer character. The difference between these three drafts is even more apparent when the number of *intersecting points* in the repeat is counted. Each time the weft passes between the warp threads from one end of the fabric to the other, it is counted as an intersecting point. In the same way the intersecting points may be counted each time a warp thread passes between the weft from the right to the wrong side of the weave or from the wrong side to the right side. Draft D has, therefore, two *ip* (intersecting points) at every eight threads, N has four, and P has six *ip* at every eight threads. Fig. 47 clearly shows that a fabric woven according to draft D would have more threads per inch in warp and weft than would be the case in draft N, and that if draft P were used, the result would be a more spaced set than in either of the foregoing.

The *angle* of the diagonal depends upon the set of the warp in relation to the set of the weft. When both have the same set, the angle is at 45°. The warp is often set somewhat more closely than the weft, giving the diagonal a more upright angle. The opposite relationship of a closer weft and a less acute angle is most unusual.

The direction of the *twist* of the warp and weft yarns affects the appearance of twill weaves, either by accentuating the diagonal or by making it less noticeable. If the fabric is to have a clearly defined diagonal, the direction of the twist of the warp and weft yarns should be opposite to the direction of the twill diagonal. A right-hand twill should therefore have a left, so-called S-twist warp yarn and a right, so-called Z-twist weft yarn (Fig. 48). If, on the other hand, a faint diagonal is desired, the diagonal and the yarn twist should go in the same direction.

The basic twills are used for a great many different fabrics. Multiple-harness twills are less frequently used as basic weaves than as the basis for the derivative weaves, particularly those with reversed drafts.

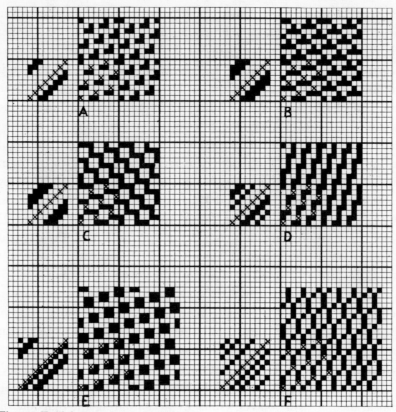

Fig. 50. Twill drafts with transposed satin.

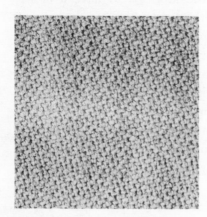

Weave based on Fig. 50 C.

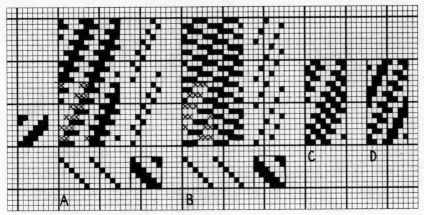

Fig. 51. Whipcord drafts.

Enlarged twills

The enlarged twills are derived from their basic weaves in the same way that rep and basket weaves are developed from tabby, by doubling of warp or weft or doubling of both warp and weft.

Fig. 49 A shows an enlarged four-harness Batavia. Every weft in the basic twill draft at the left has been doubled in the enlarged twill. The warp floats are thus longer and the structure of the weave looser than in the basic weave. A fabric in this weave can

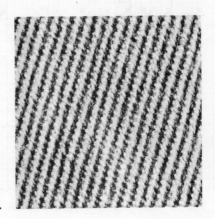

Weave based on Fig. 51 A.

71

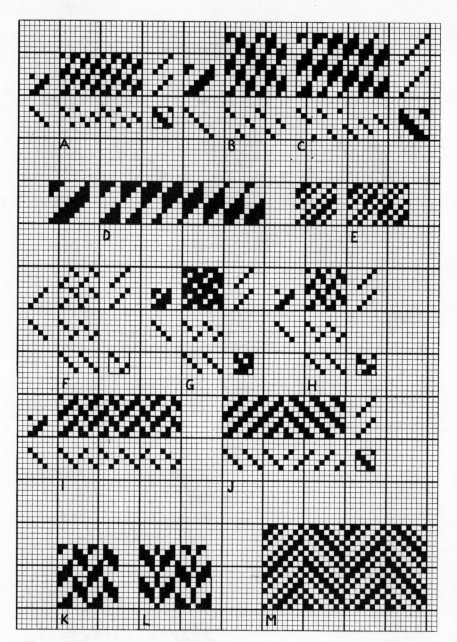

Fig. 52. Broken and broken-reversed twills.

Upholsteries in broken-reversed twills. (Swedish Handcrafts Society.)

have a closer set in the reed and become a warmer material. It is excellent as a heavy coat material, and is also frequently used in gabardine. Fig. 49 B is a $\frac{2}{1}$ twill with both warp and weft threads doubled. C has the same basic draft, but with every second warp and weft thread doubled. This is called "diagonal basket weave."

Transposed twills

New twill weaves are also obtained through the transposing, repeating or regrouping of warp and weft. Transposition may be done in irregular fashion, but better results are usually achieved if a definite plan is worked out. The transposition is made directly in the pattern diagram or by means of a draft. The methods for

73

Curtain material in 6-harness Batavia, broken and reversed both in the warp and weft.

transposing warp threads may also apply to the weft threads, and the possibilities for variations are limitless.

Fig. 50 A–F (cf. satin, p. 89), show twill weaves which have been derived from transposed satin. The basic twill is shown at the left and the twill order ×-marked. The derived twill is seen at the right with the satin order ×-marked. The satin order in A is: 1, 4, 7, 2, 5, 8, 3, 6 and the twill order: 1, 2, 3, 4, 5, 6, 7, 8. Compare the first (bottom line of Fig. 50) basic weft with the first weft in the derived weave, the fourth basic weft with the second weft in the derived weave, the seventh with the third, etc. Weaves B and F resemble crêpe weaves, and C is a diagonal basket weave. They are all drafted in consecutive order; A to D threading and treadling 1, 2, 3, 4, 5, 6, 7, 8; E and F threading and treadling 1, 2, 3, 4, 5, 6, 7, 8, 9, 10. These weaves may be used for curtains, upholstery materials, etc.

Whipcord is shown in Fig. 51 A–D. In Fig. A and B, the transposition is done by shading the wefts in a six-harness Batavia twill in the transposed repeat, as follows (numbering the wefts of the basic weaves from the bottom row): 1, 2, 3, 4, 5, 6. In this order, on draft A, every odd row is shaded, beginning with the first basic weft as the first weft in the transposed repeat. Then "×" every even row, beginning with the sixth basic weft as the second weft in

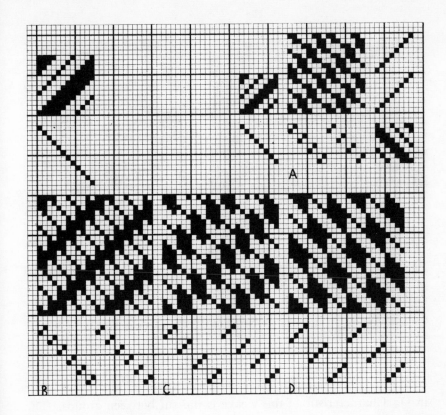

Fig. 53. Regrouped twills.

the transposed repeat. The treadling order is thus: 1, 6, 2, 1, 3, 2, 4, 3, 5, 4, 6, 5. In B, the basic wefts are shaded in the same way on the odd rows as in A. But in this instance, the even rows are "×"-d beginning with the fourth basic weft as the second in the transposed repeat. The treadling for B is as follows: 1, 4, 2, 5, 3, 6, 4, 1, 5, 2, 6, 3. The basic weave in C and D is a twill $\frac{1\ 3}{2\ 2}$. Whipcord is used for riding habits and other worsted sports clothes.

Broken twills, Fig. 52 A–E, are characterized by the transposing of the warp threads in groups. There are two warp threads in

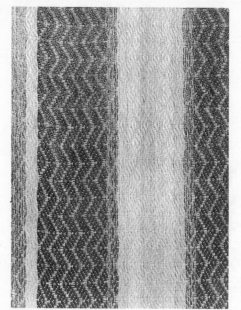

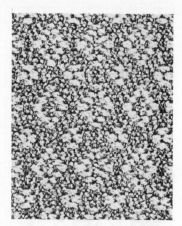

Upholstery material in regrouped pointed twill.

Drapery using draft B treadled in consecutive order and reverse.

each group in A and B; three warp threads in C and E, and four in D. Characteristic of this weave is the cut between groups. The last warp thread in one group weaves directly opposite to the first thread in the adjoining group. In other words, when the last warp thread in a group is lowered, the first thread in the next group is raised, or vice versa. In general, a Batavia is selected as the basic

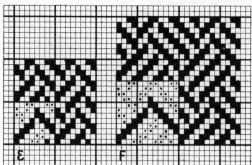

Plaited twills.

Fabric in plaited twill.

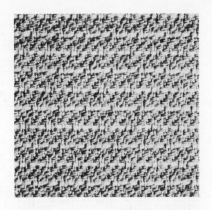

Upholstery material in plaited twill. Warp: linen 20/3. Weft: double wound wool. Reed: 12–13 dents per inch, 2 threads in a dent.

twill, but even in a twill as in E, the cut may be obtained, because the threads in the first half of the repeat weave directly opposite to the threads in the second half of the repeat.

Drapery in pointed twill. (Handcrafts Society of Borås, Sweden.)

77

Fig. 54. Pointed twills.

To draft this twill, the basic weave is drawn at left with its consecutive threading draft. The broken twill is drafted at the right following this rule: after each threaded group, skip a number of harnesses equal to half the repeat of the basic weave, minus one.

78

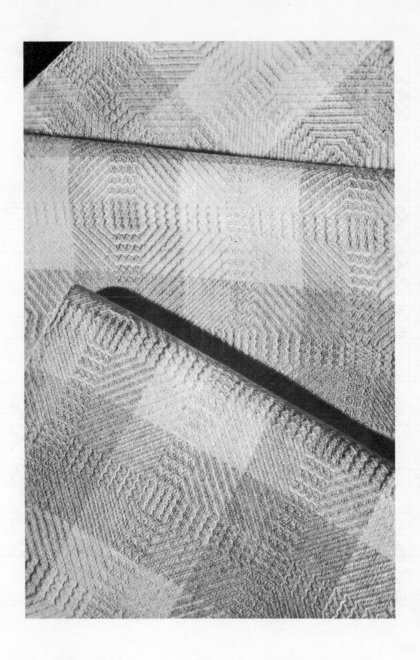

Linen table cloth in diamond twill. (Society of Friends of Handwork.)

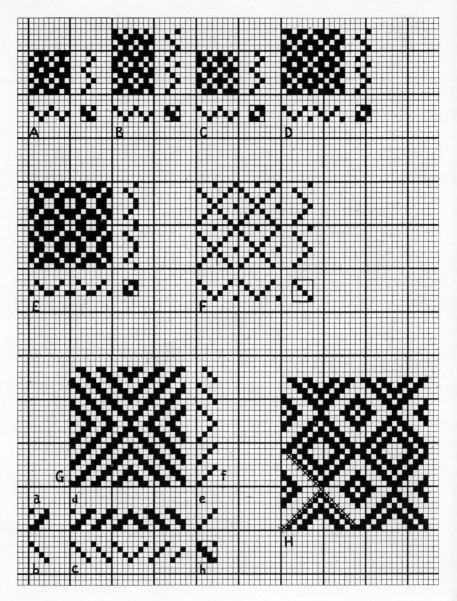

Fig. 55[1]. Diamond twills.

Thus we have in Fig. 52 A the threading 1, 2 (skip harness 3), 4, 1, (skip harness 2) 3, 4 (skip harness 1) 2, 3. After skipping harness 4, the end of the repeat is reached and we start again: 1, 2, 4, 1, 3, 4, 2, 3. Compare B and C, where a six-harness Batavia is used and two harnesses are skipped.

Broken-reversed twills differ from the foregoing in that every other group is a right diagonal and the alternating group, a left diagonal. (Fig. 52 F–M). The same rule as above applies to the threading, with this difference, that every other group is threaded in reversed order.

Among these weaves are the frequently used cross and herringbone twills. The four-harness cross twills in Fig. 52 F and G are non-reversible. F is warp-faced and G weft-faced. The distribution of binding points gives the fabric a smooth surface, reminiscent of satin weave. Cross twills are used in upholstery and linen fabrics, as well as others.

Fig. 52 H is a reversible four-harness cross twill Batavia. It is used chiefly for woolen sports fabrics. The narrow striping made by the cut should be warp-wise, in order to give the fabric good draping qualities. (See Fig. 129 B and D, regarding intersecting points.)

In Fig. 52 F, G, and H, the threading and treadling may be in consecutive order, the reversal being carried out in the treadle tie-up, as shown on the plan.

When the number of warp threads in each group is increased, the stripes become wider. Fig. 52 J illustrates this and is known as a herringbone twill. It resembles the ordinary pointed twill (Fig. 54 D), and is preferable for suiting material. In the ordinary pointed twill the floats are longer at the turning point of the diagonal, whereas in the herring-bone twill there is a cut between the stripes. Fig. 52, K, L, and M show additional examples of broken-reversed twills.

Regrouped twill weaves (Fig. 53 A–D) are also drawn down with the aid of the threading draft. For example, in a twelve-harness

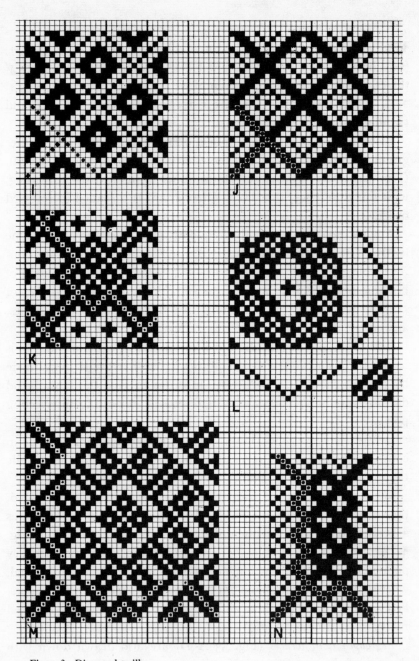

Fig. 55². Diamond twills.

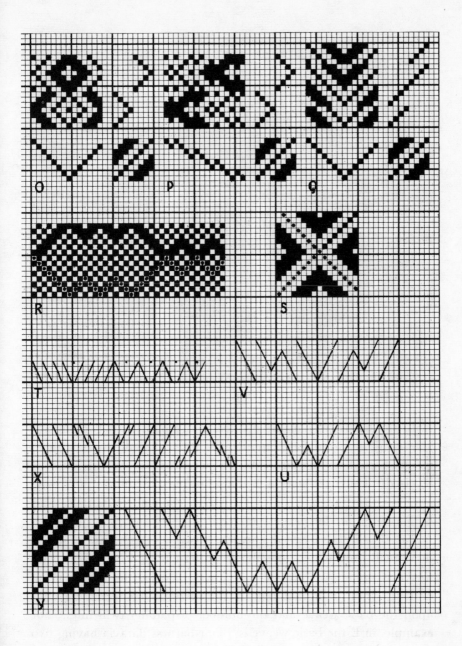

Fig. 55³. Diamond twills.

Cloth with weave Fig. 55 J developed according to V. Warp and weft: natural linen no. 20. Reed: 25 dents per inch, 2 threads in a dent. Or 16 dents per inch with 3 ends per dent.

twill, the harnesses may be divided into groups with two threads in each group, into four groups with three threads, or into three groups with four threads. Within every group the threading is reversed. Thus we have in B the following threading draft: 2–1, 4–3, 6–5, 8–7, 10–9, 12–11. Twill A is common in suitings, and B–D appropriate for drapery materials.

Plaited twill (also called entwining twill). Diagrams E and F show twill lines which resemble a pattern of plaiting. The basic weave is usually a four- or six-harness Batavia, the weave being drafted within a limited repeat. The size of the repeat depends upon the basic weave and the number of parallel twill lines. For example, in E the basic weave is a four-harness Batavia having two parallel twill lines and requiring eight warp and eight weft threads.

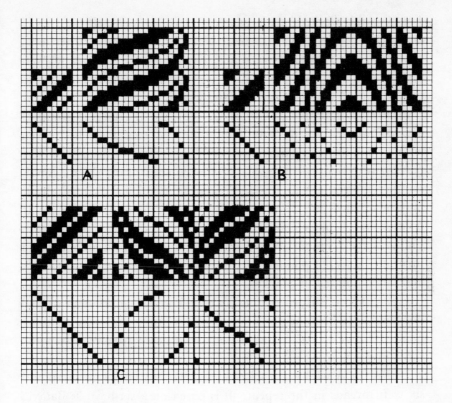

Fig. 56. Wavy twills.

Weave using draft Fig. 56 C.

The weave is worked out in consecutive order with eight harnesses and eight treadles. In F the basic weave is also a four-harness one, but with three parallel lines and having twelve warp and weft threads in the repeat, twelve harnesses and twelve treadles. Plaited twills are used for suitings, upholsteries and draperies.

Pointed twills, *striped* and *diamond*, comprise the largest group of derived weaves. Rich and handsome patterns may be woven without requiring a large number of harnesses or treadles. The pattern is developed by means of the pointed draft, the diagonals slanting alternately to the right and to the left. Pointed drafts may be divided into three main types: the simple, double or treble pointed, the broken pointed, and the fancy pointed. Examples in Fig. 54 show a simple pointed threading in draft C, double pointed in draft D, treble pointed in draft E, broken pointed in draft B, and fancy pointed in draft F.

Fig. 54 shows striped pointed twills. The weave becomes striped horizontally when the threading is consecutive and the treadling pointed (cf. Fig. 54 A and B), and vertically striped when the threading is pointed and the treadling consecutive (C–F).

In Fig. 54 A we have a four-harness Batavia with four warp and six weft threads in the repeat. B is based on a six-harness Batavia with six warp and twelve weft threads in the repeat. C is based

on a $\frac{3}{1}$ twill with six warp and four weft threads in the repeat.

To simplify this procedure, we will give the number of warp threads first and the weft threads next, and distinguish between the basic twill repeat and the pattern repeat. Thus, we have in D, the basic repeat 4 × 4, the pattern repeat 14 × 4; in E, the basic repeat 5 × 5, the pattern repeat 30 × 5; in F, the basic repeat 8 × 8, the pattern repeat 34 × 8. The weave never requires more harnesses and treadles than are needed for the basic weave (cf. drafts).

Diamond twills are shown in Fig. 55 A–Y. They differ from the striped twills in that the threading as well as the treadling is pointed either in the same or in different order. Fig. 55 A is a diamond developed from a $\frac{1}{2}$ basic twill. The pattern repeat includes four warp and four weft threads. The difference between A and C is that for the first weft in A, the first and second warp threads are lowered and the third is raised, while in C, the first thread is raised and the second and third lowered, and thus, because of a different tie-up, the patterns are unlike. When comparing B to A, it is clear that the treadling makes the difference. In C and D the difference is caused by threading and treadling. E shows that the method of increasing some threads may be used. Every thread on the third harness is doubled, as are the corresponding wefts.

Fig. 55 F shows an often used diamond twill, which in Swedish is called *korndräll*. This is based on a non-reversible four-harness twill. The pattern repeat is 8 × 8 with both threading and treadling drafts in broken pointed twill. Another and more richly patterned *korndräll* may be seen in T.

G is the so-called "goose-eye" pattern. The basic weave here is four-harness Batavia with treble-pointed threading and treadling drafts. The pattern diagram shows how the diamond twill is constructed. Start with the Batavia at left *a*, its consecutive draft *b* and the pointed draft *c*. Continue by shading in the pointed twill *d*, following the rule that every thread on harness one at *c* weaves like the first thread at *a*, every thread on the second harness weaves like the second thread at *a*, and so on. The pointed twill has a consecutive treadling *e*, and above this, the pointed treadling *f*. The diamond twill can now be shaded in by following the rule that every weft thread on treadle one in the order *f*, weaves like the first or bottom weft thread at *d*; every weft on the second treadle weaves like the second weft at *d*, etc. Fill in the pattern G, and complete the entire diagram with the tie-up plan at *h*. A suggestion may be made to try to shade in the same pattern without looking in the book. In this way, complicated patterns may be made and the construction helps one to understand how the weave is built up.

The weaves H–Q are all based on the same eight-harness twill, illustrating the possibilities of variation. They are all threaded on eight harnesses and treadled on eight treadles.

Fig. 55 H, I and J are all single pointed in both directions, and yet the patterns are different. They differ just as A and C differ, namely, in the manner of beginning the basic repeat. Compare how the warp is lowered and raised for the first weft in the three weaves: H, $\dfrac{1\ 3}{2\ 2}$, I, $\dfrac{2\ 2}{1\ 3}$, J, $\dfrac{2\ 2}{2\ 1\ 1}$. The dots within the pattern repeat help to show the construction. The draft and tie-up are worked out according to the rules already given.

In Fig. 55 K–N, the drafts are fancy pointed twills, in which no more than eight harnesses and treadles are required. The order in K is as follows: 5, 6, 7, 8, 7, 6, 5, 4, 3, 2, 1, 2, 3, 4, 3, 2, 1, 2, 3, 4, 5, 6, 7, 8, 7, 6. The basic twill repeat begins on the fourth warp and weft threads. In M, N and R the basic repeat is again at the lower left corner, with dots to give an idea of construction and draft.

O and Q are examples of smaller patterns using broken and pointed drafts and are particularly well-suited to upholstery fabrics.

Fig. 55 S is known by the name "partridge eye."

The short drafts T–Y offer further suggestions. They can be combined with different basic twills and usually the same order is used for both warp and weft.

Draft X is called "rose wreath." Y, with the draft at the right, is the "oakleaf garland," a very handsome weave which is too large to be reproduced here.

Wavy twills (Fig. 56 A–C) are distinguished from other twills, since the diagonals are not straight but follow curves. This is accomplished by the arrangement of single, double or more threads in turn, or by skipping certain harnesses. The results will be weaves with fairly long floats and will be best suited for such fabrics as drapery materials.

SATIN WEAVES

Regular satin weaves

These weaves are non-reversible and have one binding point only on each warp thread within the repeat (Fig. 57 A–Ä). In a *warp-faced satin*, one warp thread is lowered for each weft, and in a *weft-faced satin*, one warp thread is raised for each weft. The binding points are distributed in such a way that they never adjoin one another, and thus the fabric attains a smooth, glossy surface.

To distribute the binding points, a regular sequence is followed: Fig. 57 D illustrates the construction of a *regular* five-harness warp-faced satin. Here the sequence 1, 3, 5, 2, 4 is used. Begin by filling in the square in the lower left-hand corner, indicating that the

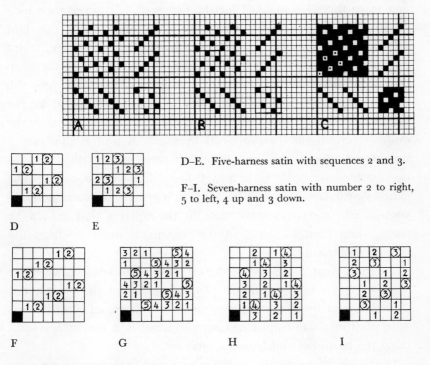

D–E. Five-harness satin with sequences 2 and 3.

F–I. Seven-harness satin with number 2 to right, 5 to left, 4 up and 3 down.

D E

F G H I

Fig. 57[1]. Satin weaves.

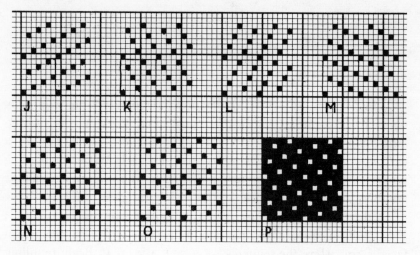

Fig. 57². Satin weaves.

first warp thread is lowered for the first weft. To ascertain which warp thread is lowered for the second weft, count 1, 2 to the right and fill in the square on the third thread. For weft three, count 1, 2 and shade in the fifth thread. Since this is the end of the warp repeat, begin counting from the first warp thread, shading the second thread, for weft four, and finally, the fourth thread for the fifth weft. At D, the system of construction is shown and at A the draft is carried out in the usual manner. E and B illustrate a warp-faced weave, this time counting three rather than two, as previously described. C is a weft-faced five-harness satin. The easiest way to construct weft-faced satins is to mark the corresponding warp-faced satin with small dots in the squares that should be empty, and then to shade in the remaining squares within the repeat. Compare C to A.

All satin weaves are threaded and treadled in consecutive order (Fig. 57 A–C) and the tie-up plan is similar to the repeat, but turned diagonally in the opposite direction. Thus, an eight-harness satin is set up using eight harnesses and treadles, a ten-harness satin using ten harnesses and treadles, etc.

In the five-harness satin we have employed the sequence numbers

90

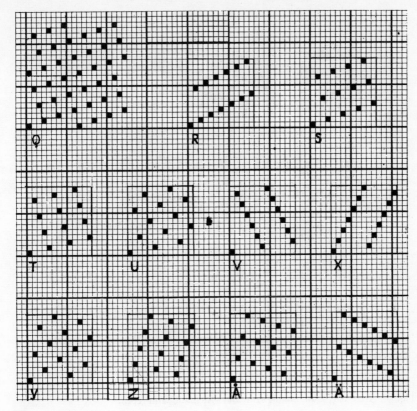

Fig. 57³. Satin weaves.

two and three in constructing drafts. Number One cannot be used since it produces a twill weave (cf. Fig. 45 G). For the same reason the number of threads in a repeat minus one $(5 - 1 = 4)$ cannot be used. Also, it is not possible to use a number equal to the number of threads in a repeat. In addition, a number which is a factor of the number of threads in the repeat, or a multiple of that factor, cannot be used. The underlined figures in the table indicate which ones may be used in constructing satins. From this table it is evident that 5×5 squares are required. In fact, the five-harness satin is most widely used.

A *regular* six-harness satin cannot be constructed, since in the number-group: 1, 2, 3, 4, 5 and 6, numbers 1, 5 and 6 are out; and 2, 3 and 4 are factors, or multiples.

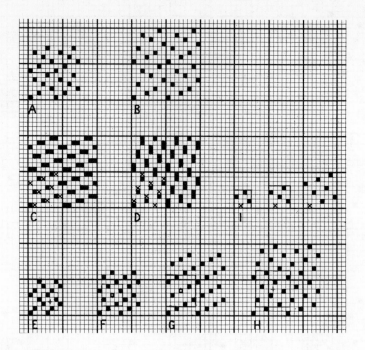

Fig. 58. Irregular, satin, double satin and systematic satin repeats.

Within the repeat 7 × 7, sequence numbers two, three, four or five (Fig. 57 F–M) can be used. No matter which number we choose, the weave will be the same. But compare J, K, L and M and observe that the diagonal lines run in opposite directions and that the binding points lie closer to each other in one direction

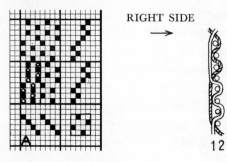

RIGHT SIDE
→

Fig. 59. Rep with floats bound on the reverse side. Cross section of weft at the first two warp threads in A.

12

than in the other. These lines are called *false twill* and do not appear in the five-harness satin or in satins Q and U. The latter weaves are called *square satins*. Fig. 57 F, G, H and I show that the same results may be obtained whether the graph is filled in to the right, to the left, upwards or downwards.

The eight-harness satins N–P are used for closely set fabrics and damasks. The ten-harness satin Q is a square satin.

Fig. 57 R–Ä are examples which show that when more than four numbers may form the sequence, different satin weaves can be constructed using the same number of threads in the repeat. For example, here is a thirteen-harness satin in which ten numbers may be used to construct three different satins. R, V and Ä have marked twill lines; S, T, Z and Å are alike; U and Y are square satins. They are seldom used as satins, but their sequence may be used in twill derivations and crêpe weaves.

In a satin fabric, the scattered binding points are to a great extent concealed by the floats on either side. For this reason a satin weave may have a closer set than a twill weave having the same number of intersections.

Irregular satin weaves

Irregular satins are usually constructed on six or eight harnesses, as illustrated in Fig. 58 A and B. They give a somewhat livelier texture than the five-harness satin and are often used in upholstery fabrics.

Double satin weaves

Double satins (Fig. 58 C and D) are used both to shorten the floats in ordinary satin and to facilitate shed forming when weaving jacquard designs. The additional binding points are located beside or above the satin points.

There are actually no derivatives of the satin weave, as satin

93

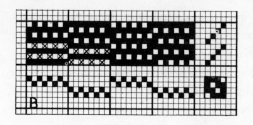

1   Cross section of warp at the first two
                                         wefts in B.

itself is regarded as a transposed twill. The only weaves which
might be so considered are *dräll* and damask, but as they are constructed, using a combination of warp-faced and weft-faced satins,
or of some other non-reversible weave, they are dealt with under
the heading of combined weaves.

Systematic satin repeats

For such combinations, the *systematic satin repeats* are used. These
have the binding points evenly distributed around a central point
(Fig. 58 F–H). As the cross twill in E is often used in the same way
as the satin, a systematic repeat is also shown. For this cross twill
and for five- and eight-harness satins, there is a rule for obtaining
the systematic repeats (see I). They all commence with the point
in the second square. In the last two weaves, sequence number
Three is used.

VARIED REP WEAVES

Rep with a tabby reverse side

In an earlier chapter on rep weaves we have described how a
fabric may have a firmer character if additional binding threads

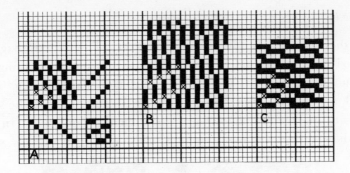

Fig. 60. Diagonal rep weaves.

are inserted between the rep threads. These threads are completely concealed, and the fabric is still reversible. Another method of binding the rep is to cause the floats on the reverse side to weave in tabby, while the floats on the right side remain unchanged (Fig. 59 A–B).

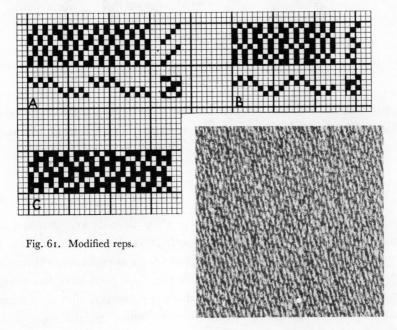

Fig. 61. Modified reps.

Upholstery using pattern A.

Diagonal rep weaves

In these weaves the stripes run diagonally. The pattern diagram is filled in with the aid of the satin weave system, and using an odd number of harnesses. In the warp diagonal reps in Fig. 60 A and B, a sufficient number of squares are shaded in above the satin points to make the longest warp floats on the right side. In the weft diagonal rep, as many squares are shaded in beside the satin

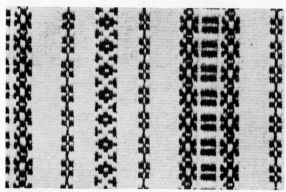

Detail of a runner in rosepath. Warp: linen 20/3. Weft: wool single for background, double wool for rosepath. Reed: 12–13 dents per inch with 1 thread in a dent.

points as will bring about the longest weft floats on the right side. Fig. 60 A can be used as any twill might be, and B and C are good for suitings.

Modified rep weaves

These are obtained when the rep warp threads are graphed in groups commencing on different wefts. In Fig. 61 A the warp rep 2/2 changes its position in the second weft after six warp threads, and in B, the warp rep 3/1 moves in the third weft after five warp threads. C shows a warp rep 4/4 which is staggered after four warp threads and in addition, is more closely bound on the right side. This is used as a fine wool suiting.

96

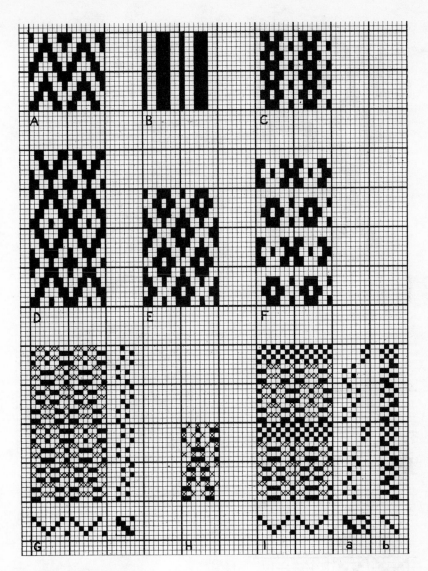

Fig. 62. Rosepath.

Cross section of warp at first and second wefts in G.

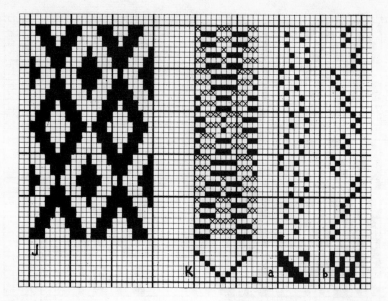

Six-harness rosepath.

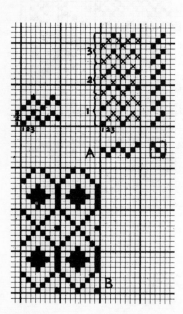

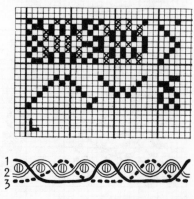

Cross section of warp threads in the first 3 wefts in A.

Fig. 63. Bound rosepath.

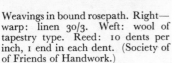

Weavings in bound rosepath. Right—
warp: linen 30/3. Weft: wool of
tapestry type. Reed: 10 dents per
inch, 1 end in each dent. (Society of
of Friends of Handwork.)

Rosepath

Weaves known as rosepath may be placed in two general classifications: "ordinary rosepath" woven on opposites, and "bound rosepath." Both types are distinguished by their rich variety of patterns and colors. The weaver often improvises in such a way that the patterns may be different from beginning to end. Rosepath is also woven in bands with tabby and rep stripes between.

Ordinary rosepath, woven on opposites, is one of our most common art weaves. Fig. 62 A–F illustrate some patterns which frequently recur in the patterns, such as points, stripes, squares and "roses." These designs can be derived from four-harness Batavia twill, but rosepath can also be woven with six- and even eight-harness Batavia motifs.

99

Fig. 62 G is the pattern diagram of design A. Rosepath is woven with two shuttles and a weft shot in one color is followed by a contrasting color in the opposite shed. In G, two wefts and two opposite wefts are woven before the pattern rep shifts. In this way the weft covers the warp and a patterned weft-faced rep is obtained (see cross-section). The fabric is equally interlaced on the right and reverse sides.

Broken point threading, so-called V-point, is most common, and the tie-up is like that of the Batavia twill. The treadle draft, however, will vary in each design.

Wefts on opposites are sometimes replaced by tabby (see H), and are considered a variation of rosepath.

The pattern diagram I carries out design F, where bands of rosepath alternate with tabby bands. The tabby wefts require extra treadles, as in *a*. If there are only four treadles on the loom, tie-up plan *b* can be used and two treadles will have to be depressed for each weft.

Fig. 62 J and K show a design and pattern diagram for six-harness rosepath. In the tie-up plan *b* opposite treadles have been placed beside each other, to facilitate treadling.

When weaving rosepath, lock one yarn weft around its opposite weft at the selvedges, so that they bind at the edges. In beginning or ending a weft shot, care should be taken not to lay yarns of different colors in the same shed.

Ordinary rosepath has many uses today, as in upholsteries, pillow tops, table cloths, rugs, dress materials, aprons, etc. When rosepath is used in curtain and drapery materials, the pattern is often placed in the direction of the warp. In this "lengthwise rosepath," the ordinary threading becomes the treadling, and the treadling, the threading. The set of the weft becomes the set of the warp, and the fabric warp-faced instead of weft-faced.

In *bound rosepath* the pattern is derived from a non-reversible twill, usually with three or four harnesses. The patterns may be varied to a great extent and woven in many colors.

Fig. 63 A is a simple pattern using three harnesses and pointed threading, and B is a pattern for four harnesses with broken pointed threading. One harness is always tied to each treadle.

Bound rosepath is a peculiar type of weave, its pattern being formed in a completely different way from that of ordinary rosepath. The pattern diagram looks like a pointed twill with its treadling draft in consecutive order. But the character of a twill disappears in the weave, since the warp is widely set and the weft is closely woven, which gives the fabric a rep-like surface and conceals the warp.

Every squared row in the pattern at left (Fig. 63 A) represents six shots of weft, each warp thread thus corresponding to six wefts (diagram at right). On the face side of the fabric the weft floats are never over more than one warp thread at a time, but on the reverse side the weft floats are under several threads. The fabric is, therefore, non-reversible with a clear pattern tightly woven on the face side and with a looser weave on the reverse side.

Treadling for all patterns is in consecutive order, the pattern appearing through color variations. In three-harness bound rosepath three wefts of different colors may simultaneously develop a pattern, and on a four-harness set-up, four differently colored wefts may be used.

Bound rosepath has been used chiefly for cushions and similar coverings.

Rep rugs

Rep rugs have a closely set warp in two or more colors and a weft consisting of alternating heavy and fine yarns. The weave is somewhat like a warp rep 3/1. The patterns are the same as those in *dräll* weaves and comprise two, three or four blocks. (For *dräll* patterns, block patterns, short drafts, see p. 122.)

For each pattern block the warp is threaded on two harnesses with one color on the odd harness and the other on the even harness. For example, if the warp is red and white, the harnesses can be

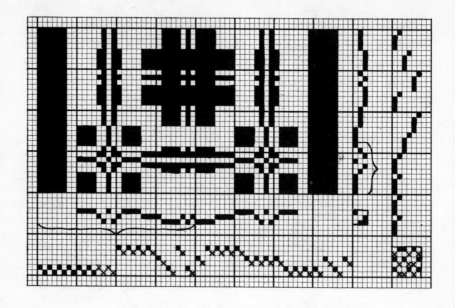

Fig. 64. Pattern for rep rug.

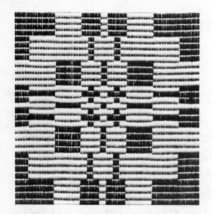

Detail of rep. rug.

102

tied to the treadles in such a way that the red threads are raised in one block and the white in all the others. The threads which are raised over the heavy weft yarn form the main pattern effect, while the fine weft yarn serves to bind the threads between the heavy wefts.

When the pattern has been sketched in and supplied with a short draft, the threading, tie-up and treadling can be worked out directly from it.

The *extended threading draft* is based on the short draft. If the rug has a plain border, this is threaded on the block having the least number of threads.

Each pattern block requires two treadles, one of which is tied to the odd harness and the other to the even harness. A shaded square in the short treadle tie-up draft indicates that the even harness is depressed, while the blank square indicates that the odd harness is depressed. This rule applies to the odd treadles which are used for the heavy weft. The even treadles are tied entirely opposite to the odd treadles.

In the treadling draft the pattern blocks are developed according to the short draft treadling plan.

Fig. 64 illustrates a rep rug in a three-block pattern with borders, and Fig. 65 a rug in two blocks with borders. The latter may be threaded in different ways because the two blocks are the opposite of one another. Theoretically, this pattern can be threaded on two harnesses (b), if the colors are reversed in the second block. But since the heddles would be too crowded on the harnesses, threading on four harnesses, as in c, is preferable. It is unnecessary to have more than two treadles. The pattern blocks are changed by omitting the wefts of fine yarn.

In a four-block pattern in which the alternate blocks are opposites, the threading may be on four harnesses instead of eight.

A two-ply cotton yarn is usually used for the warp. The heavy weft yarn may be cotton roving or finely cut rags, while the fine weft is generally the same as the warp.

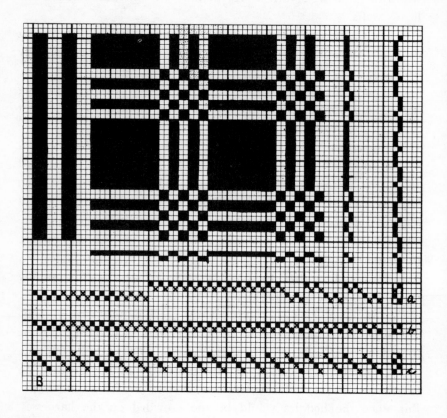

Fig. 65. Pattern for rep rug.

When making a rep rug begin and end by weaving in an inch or two of the fine weft yarn. At the selvedges the heavy and fine wefts are locked around each other to bind the outer warp thread.

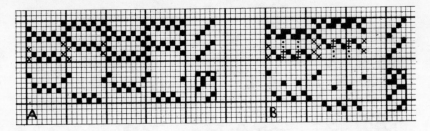

Fig. 66. Patterns for vertically striped cord weaves.

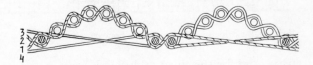

Cross section of
warp threads at
the first four
weft shots in A.

$\begin{matrix}3\\2\\1\\4\end{matrix}$

WEAVES THAT FORM UNEVEN SURFACE TEXTURES

Cord weaves (Bedford cord)

To obtain raised vertical or horizontal stripes in a fabric, the weaves in Fig. 66 A–D are used.

They are constructed in the following manner: the width of the stripes is decided upon, as for example, in Fig. 66 A, a stripe six warp threads wide. Tabby warp threads are filled in on either side of the stripe (marked with ×'s in the diagram). Between these, tabby is shaded in for the first and second wefts of the first raised

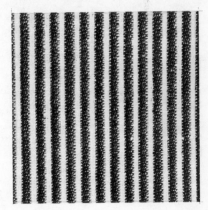

Fabric in cord weave.

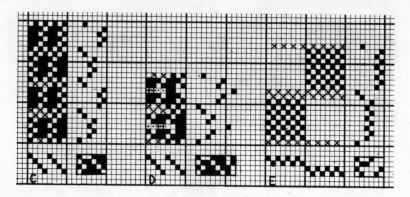

Horizontally striped cord weaves and honeycomb weave.

stripe, and for the third and fourth wefts of the second raised stripe. The wefts which lie in loose floats on the reverse side draw up the stripes, so that the tabby-weaving wefts are raised (see cross-section).

To raise the stripes even more, padding threads (Fig. 66 B) may be added, which lie within the stripes.

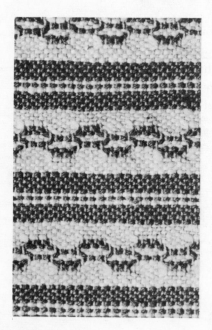

Upholstery fabric with stripes in honeycomb weave.

Upholstery fabrics using honeycomb weaves. The fabric at left is woven with two colors in warp and weft of cotton 30/2 and intermediate wefts of unbleached linen no. 10. Reed: 18 dents per inch, 2 ends in a dent. The right-hand fabric is woven with cotton 16/2 in the warp and 2 colors of cottolin 6/2 in the weft. Reed: 23 dents per inch, 1 end in a dent.

Fig. 66 C shows a horizontally striped weave, while D is similar, but with padding wefts.

The above weaves are commonly used in suitings, cotton fabrics and even as upholstery materials. Machine-woven cottons in cord weave are inappropriately called piqué; a true piqué is a double weave.

Honeycomb

Honeycomb (*hålkrus*) is very much like the foregoing, except that it is in the form of squares (Fig. 66 E). When woven in more elaborate patterns, it is known, in Swedish, as "*Gagnefkrus*" (F).

In constructing honeycomb, first fill in the all-tabby wefts which are spaced at intervals from one another. (In Fig. E these are eight wefts apart and are indicated by ×'s.) Then shade in with tabby the first pattern square between the first and second all-tabby (×'ed) wefts. Next shade in the second pattern square between the third and fourth all-tabby wefts. In the weave, these all-tabby

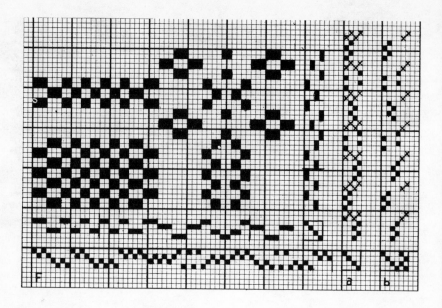

Pattern in *"gagnefkrus"* with short and extended drafts. In the short-threading draft, one square represents 2 threads, see squares 15 to 45. Two squares in the short treadling draft represent 6 wefts, see squares 9 to 22.

wefts are brought together over the loosely bound square, drawing the tabby pattern square together so that it forms a round depression.

There are usually two tabby wefts between the depressed squares, although sometimes only one weft shot is made. Often a heavier yarn is used for these wefts than is used for the squares.

Fig. 66 F is a pattern in *Gagnefkrus*. As the pattern diagram would be too large to show here in detail, merely the basic principles are given.

The pattern consists of four blocks (cf. *dräll*, p. 122). It is threaded on four harnesses with the first block threaded on harnesses one and two, the second block on harnesses three and two, the third block on harnesses three and four, and the fourth block on harnesses one and four. The harnesses are tied to four treadles as in tie-up

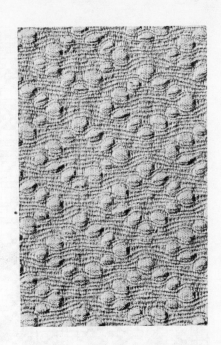

Upholstery in honeycomb weave.

plan *a*, or to six treadles, as in plan *b*. When weaving the depressed pattern squares, two treadles are used alternately, always beginning with the odd one. Two tabby shots are woven between the squares (cf. E).

Observe that the squares in the lower left section of the pattern are in the first and third blocks of the short draft, and are threaded on opposite harnesses in the extended draft.

Gagnefkrus weave derives its name from its use in the national costume worn in the parish of Gagnef in Dalecarlia, Sweden. Honeycomb, and the more elaborate *Gagnefkrus*, are used for bedspreads and upholstery fabrics.

Waffle weave

Waffle weaves are made up of warp- and weft-faced diamonds, between which run diagonal tabby lines (Fig. 67 A–D). The long

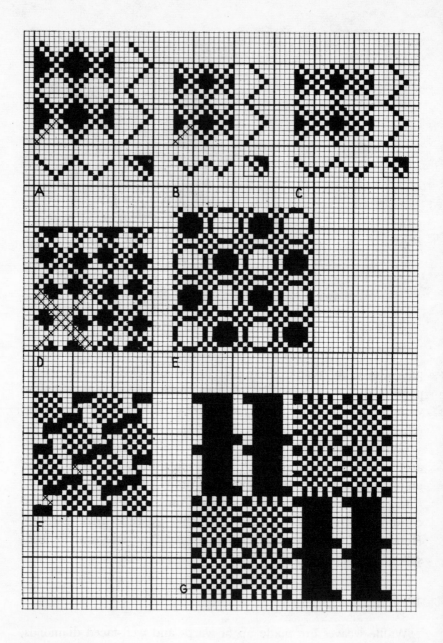

Fig. 67. Waffle weaves.

Weaves using drafts A, F and G.

Table cloth in lace weave checks. Warp and weft semi-bleached and colored linen No. 20, 2 ends in each heddle. Reed: 20 dents per inch, 2 ends in each dent.

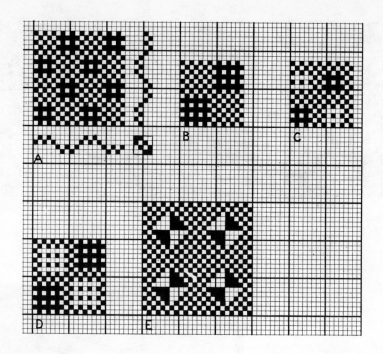

Fig. 68. Huckaback weaves.

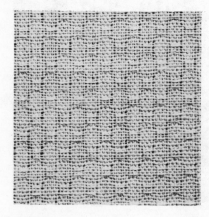

Fabric in huckaback weave A.

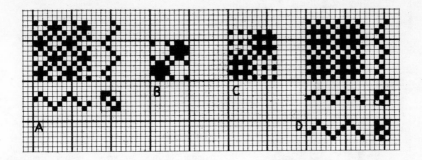

Fig. 69. Open weaves.

warp and weft floats tend to draw the fabric together, while the closely woven tabby areas tend to extend it. In this way, ridges and depressions are formed. Warp and weft floats which run vertically and horizontally give a squared effect to the weave.

Fig. 67 A is an example of one of the most common waffle weaves using five harnesses and six treadles, and a pointed draft. B and C are waffle weaves using four harnesses and five treadles, and D is a waffle weave variation with twelve harnesses and treadles.

These weaves are used for linen or cotton towels, for light-weight woolens, cotton fabrics, bedspreads, etc.

Huckaback weaves

Huckaback is a tabby weave, which at regular intervals is broken by floats over groups of threads (Fig. 68 A–E). These floats may be either in the warp or the weft, or in both alternately.

Huckaback also occurs in pattern combinations, such as in "Halland huck," woven according to draft A, or in "seventh-jump huck," draft B. Draft D is called "Greek huck." It differs from the above in that the thread which forms a long float in one pattern square binds in tabby in the next square. In this way the number of intersections are more evenly distributed.

Huckaback is a particularly good weave for towels because of

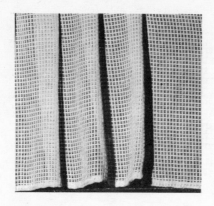

Lace weave curtain fabric (Fig. 69 D). Warp and weft: 30/2 cotton. Reed: 30 dents per inch, sleyed 2–1–2–0–1–0 ends in dents.

its textured surface. It is also a decorative weave and may be used for table cloths and upholstery fabrics. Greek huck is used for curtains and may be considered as a transition into the next group of weaves: the open weaves.

Open weaves (lace weaves)

These weaves, which give an open, lacy appearance (Fig. 69 A–D) are constructed so that thread groups bind as opposites. The

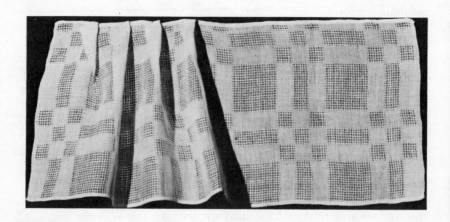

Checked lace weave curtain. Warp and weft: lines no. 50. Reed: 35 dents per inch, 1 end in each dent. (Textile Institute at Borås, Sweden.)

Left: upholstery in crêpe weave draft Fig. 70 A; wool 8/2, reed 10 dents per inch, 2 ends in a dent. Center: cotton fabric, draft H; cotton 12/2, reed 15 dents per inch, 2 ends in a dent. Right: upholstery in crêpe weave draft N; Persian wool, reed 12–13 dents per inch, 2 ends in a dent.

opposite weave causes the groups of threads to pull away from each other and thus leave openings. This applies both in the direction of the warp and of the weft.

Fig. 69 B shows the classic open weave with a double warp thread and a double weft in the center of each group.

D is the lace weave called "mosquito netting," and can be threaded on three harnesses, although it is easier to weave if threaded on four harnesses.

To aid in forming the apertures in this weave, the threads comprising a group are sleyed together in one dent, while empty dents are left between the groups. Sleying the reed for this lace weave is as follows: 5–0–0–1–0–0 threads in each dent, or 2–1–2–0–1–0 threads in each dent. Lace weave is often combined with tabby to form checked patterns. In this instance, the warp should be threaded with one thread per dent to avoid a striped appearance in the tabby square. The lacy effect will not become apparent until the fabric has been laundered. The open weaves are chiefly used for curtain materials.

Fabrics with open spaces may also be produced with ordinary tabby weave. The warp ends are simply sleyed in groups with empty

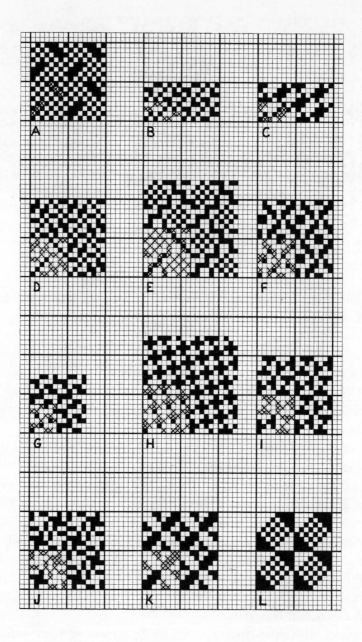

Fig. 70¹. Crêpe weaves.

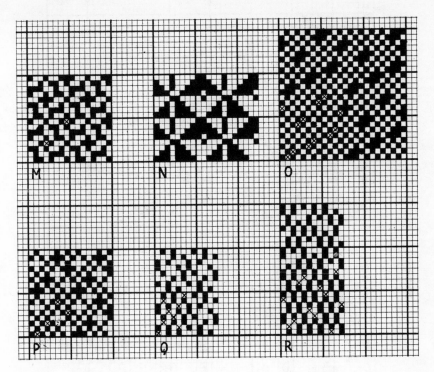

Fig. 70². Crêpe weaves.

dents between, and are woven with corresponding open areas between groups of wefts.

Crêpe weaves

A great variety of weaves fall into this category, because they have in common a lively and irregularly textured appearance. Many crêpe fabrics are of a particularly elastic character, which may be due to the construction of the weave, or to the use of crêpe-twisted yarns. A simple crêpe material can be woven in tabby with the aid of crêpe-twisted yarn.

Crêpe weaves are often constructed by a combination of two other weaves, such as tabby and twill, satin and rep, cross twill and

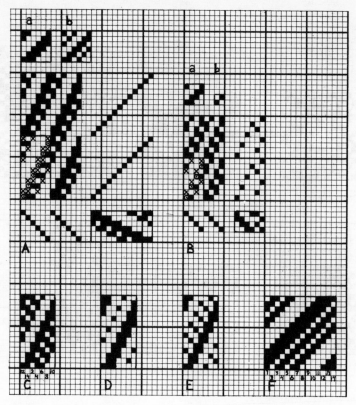

Fig. 71. Diagonal weaves.

tabby, etc., the one weave mingled with the other. This is indicated by the filled-in squares and the ×-marked squares in the repeats (Fig. 70).

Fig. 70 A shows tabby and cross twill; B, tabby and weft rep; C, pointed twill and additional points forming opposite weaving figures. D is an example of cross twill and broken twill, and E of cross twill combined with tabby and additional binding points. F is an irregular eight-harness satin with three binding points added to every warp thread, i.e., with one point directly over the satin point, one skipped, two added and three skipped. In the same way, two points are added to the irregular six-harness satin in G, and four points are added to the regular ten-harness satin in H.

118

Sports fabrics using drafts Fig. 71, C, D and E.

Drafts I–K are constructed by dividing the repeat into four squares and shading in a pattern in the lower left square. The other three squares are then completed by filling in the pattern in direct opposition to one another (observe ×'d areas). Variations of this method are given in drafts L and N.

Fig. 70 M has two center points around which S-shaped figures are placed. Draft D is based on a tabby weave to which a doubled irregular six-harness satin is added. P is also based on tabby with four binding points added in cross twill order and with four other points eliminated in the same order.

Finally, drafts Q and R are based on warp rep with eliminated points ×-marked in the first repeat.

Crêpe weaves may be classified in the following groups:

Sand crêpe—A, O, and P; mossy crêpe—B, D, E, F and M; sponge crêpe—C, G and H; opposite-weaving crêpe—I, J and K; rep crêpe—Q and R. Of these, sponge weaves have a very elastic character, while opposite weaves give firmness to a fabric.

Crêpe weaves can be used in practically all types of handwoven and machine-woven textiles. Sand crêpe is often used in machine-woven dress materials. If these textiles are Jacquard woven, much larger repeats are possible than are shown here.

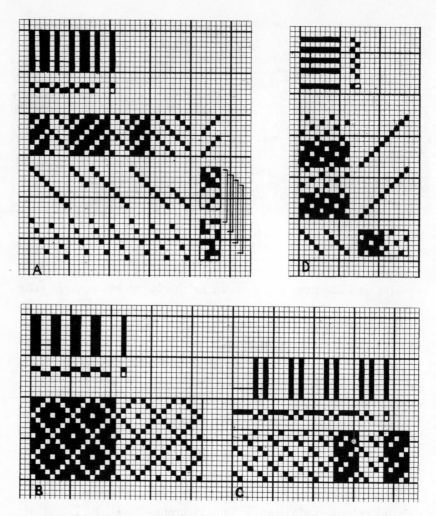

Fig. 72¹. Patterns in striped *dräll*.

The draft is usually in consecutive order with the number of harnesses required equal to the number of warp ends in the repeat. The number of treadles needed is equal to the number of wefts in the repeat. Here are some exceptions: Fig. 70 B, four harnesses and treadles with this threading: 1, 2, 3, 4, 1, 3, 2, 4, and this

Curtain material from draft C. Warp: white and colored wool 20/2. Weft: wool no. 10. Reed: 15 ends per inch, 2 ends in a dent.

treadling: 1, 2, 3, 4; Fig. 70 N, six harnesses and eight treadles with this threading: 1, 2, 3, 4, 5, 3, 2, 1, 6, 4, and the treadling in consecutive order: 1, 2, 3, 4, 5, 6, 7, 8. The tie-up plan is worked out as described in Fig. 38.

COMBINED WEAVES

Diagonal weaves

Ordinary twill weaves are frequently called diagonal weaves. However, these diagonal weaves may also be the result of a combination of twill weaves. This combination usually takes place in the direction of the weft, with one weft woven according to one basic twill and the alternate weft according to another (Fig. 71 A–F). The two basic repeats should be equal in size or equally divisible. In Fig. 71 A, the four-harness Batavia *a* is graphed on the odd wefts of the diagonal weave, and the twill in *b* (×-marked) is graphed on the even wefts.

Fig. 71 B is a four-harness Batavia combined with tabby. The Batavia or balanced twill is shaded in on the odd wefts with the tabby on the even wefts.

Fig. 71 C can be constructed in two different ways. One method

is to shade in the wefts by combining a twill $\dfrac{1\ 2}{2\ 2}$ with a twill $\dfrac{1\ 2}{3\ 1}$.
The other method is to shade in the warp threads, eliminating the odd warp threads and shading only the even warp threads in F. The even numbers below pattern F are used in C. Note, however, that the numbers are taken in this order: 12, 14, 2, 4, 6, 8, 10 in constructing pattern C. Drafts D and E are further examples of this latter method. Seven harnesses and fourteen treadles are required for drafts C, D and E.

Draft B can be used for handwoven coat materials. The other drafts serve best for worsted sports materials and uniforms.

If a warp-faced twill is combined in this manner with a weft-faced twill, a double-faced fabric is obtained (see chapter on double-faced weaves).

Dräll weaves (sometimes misnamed damask)

In *dräll* technique, a wrap-faced repeat is combined with a weft-faced repeat of the same weave. The combination is developed either as a striped or a checked pattern (Fig. 72 A–G).

Usually the weave is warp-faced satin combined with weft-faced satin. Other combinations of clear warp and weft effects, such as twill, cross twill and diamond twill, may also be used.

The floats in the areas of warp effect are exactly opposite to those in the areas of weft effect, so that when the light falls on the fabric, the areas in the one appear light, while those in the other appear somewhat darker. Yarns with high luster bring out this difference, so that the pattern becomes more marked.

To work out the draft for a particular *dräll* pattern, it is necessary first, to determine how many blocks the pattern contains, and second, what weave is to be used.

Thus, the block pattern is graphed, with every shaded square representing a weft-face repeat, and every blank square a warp-face repeat. Then a short draft is made. Each row of squares which

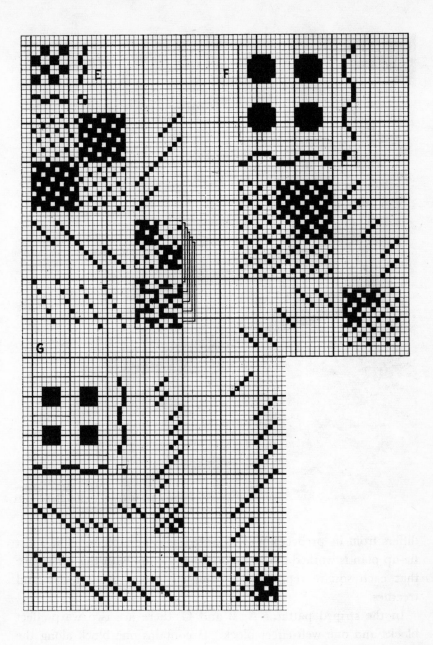

Fig. 72². Patterns for *dräll* table cloths.

123

Dräll table cloths
(Swedish Handcrafts
Society.)

differs from its predecessor is regarded as a new block. The short tie-up plan is worked out as an ordinary tie-up, with this difference that each square represents a complete group of harnesses and treadles.

In the striped patterns A, B and C, there are two warp-effect blocks and one weft-effect block. D contains one block along the warp and two along the weft.

Dräll table cloth "Night and Day." (Swedish Handcrafts Society.)

The pattern diagram is made in such a way that a definite cut divides the warp and weft-faced areas. If this is neglected, the threads in one stripe will slide over into the next stripe. In striped patterns like those in Fig. 72 A–D, the cut is produced if the warp repeat is symmetrical and opposite to the weft repeat.

In Fig. 72 A the weave is a four-harness twill. Below the pattern diagram there are two different threading drafts. In the first draft, the first block is threaded on harnesses one to four, and the second block on harnesses five to eight. In the second threading draft, the first block is threaded on the odd harnesses, and the second block on the even harnesses. The second is preferable, for there is a more even distribution of the warp threads in the shed. In the first threading draft, there would be a tendency for the threads in the first block to rise higher in the shed than those in the second block which might cause long "weft jumps" in the weave.

125

Dräll threading drafts from an old weaving book.

Fig. 72 B and C show vertically striped *dräll* patterns, and D is a horizontally striped *dräll*. The basic weaves are diamond twill, regrouped twill and satin.

Striped patterns are used chiefly for curtains and upholstery fabrics. For linen hand towels, a striped center with a checked border is often used.

Designs in checks for *dräll* table cloths are seen in Fig. 72 E–G. Draft E is called the "chess pattern," and F, the "beauty-spot." These designs merely serve as examples of how blocks and drafts are worked out from a particular pattern. When they are used for table cloths, the size of the pattern must be in proportion to the size of the cloth and the weight of the yarn to be used. In the borders there should be frequent alternations of the blocks at the edges and hems.

The pattern diagram is graphed using the systematic repeats (see Fig. 58 I). The cut between the repeats is produced if the warp-faced area is symmetrical and opposite to the weft-faced area. For example, the warp threads are raised and lowered in the first

126

Fig. 73. Detail of damask weave.   Fig. 74. Detail of Jacquard weave.

weft of the detailed draft, in Fig. 72 E, like this: weft-faced area $\frac{1\ 1}{1\ 4\ 3}$, cut, warp-faced area $\frac{3\ 4\ 1}{1\ 1}$.

Two different threadings are worked out for pattern E in the same way as for A. All patterns can be re-threaded in this way. Those which contain three blocks are threaded with the blocks on every third harness.

Fig. 72 G shows a pattern with two different suggestions for the basic weave. The first is a three-harness twill, and the second a five-harness satin. The former is easier to weave, but the latter will produce a closer, more lustrous fabric.

Damask weaves

Damask is characterized by richer and more unrestricted pattern development than can be produced in a *dräll* weave. It is, however, constructed on the same basis of contrast between warp and weft effects. In damask, the right side is usually the one in which the pattern is formed by weft floats, while the ground is in warp effect. Because damask patterns are distinguished by more elaborate designs, they cannot be woven on an ordinary loom with one set of harnesses.

127

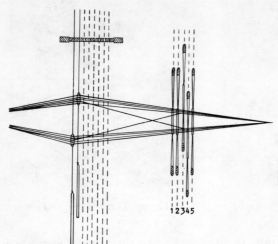

Fig. 75. In damask weaving the pattern shed and the ground shed are combined, causing certain warp threads to cross between the sheds.

Pattern shed.

Combined pattern and ground shed.

First weft.
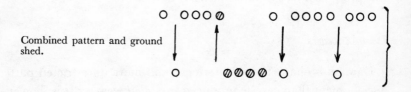

Fig. 76.

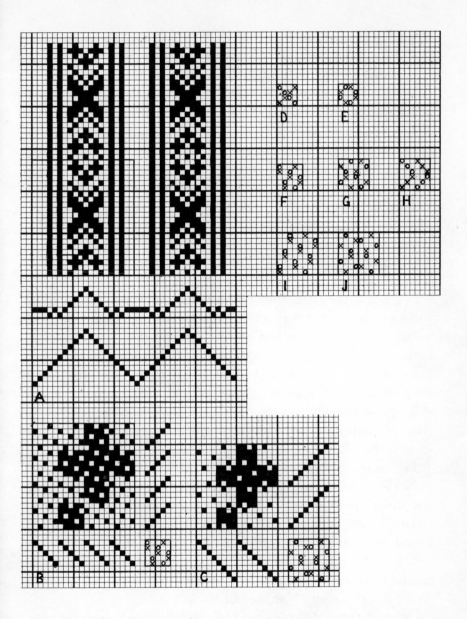

Fig. 77. Pattern for damask towel. When weaving with weaving sword, the pattern is picked up on 6 heddle sticks. In weaving on a draw-harness loom, the threading is pointed on 11 pattern harnesses.

The basic weave most commonly used in damask is five-harness satin. But twill, cross twill, irregular satin and eight-harness satin —the latter for the finest qualities—are also used.

Damask is woven most frequently in *all white* or in a *one-color* linen or silk and is used for table cloths and upholsteries.

The distinguishing feature of a damask weave, as compared to a Jacquard weave, is its step-like pattern contours. This is due, both in damasks as well as in *drälls*, to the fact that these weaves consist of units containing several warp and weft threads, thus causing the stepped outlines (Fig. 73). In the Jacquard weave, on the other hand, every warp and weft thread may bind differently, bringing about smooth, even contours (Fig. 74). Damask patterns are often of a simpler and firmer construction than those of a Jacquard weave.

Principles of damask weaving. Damask can be woven according to various methods, but they all have in common the factor that two sheds, one pattern shed and one background shed, are combined during weaving (Fig. 75). In the pattern shed a division takes place between the blocks which form the warp effect and those the weft effect. The former are raised and the latter are lowered (Fig. 76). This division may be accomplished on such different types of looms as an ordinary loom with a weaving sword, a draw loom, a draw-harness loom and a Jacquard loom.

The weave is obtained by means of the background shed. One thread from every raised repeat in the pattern shed is lowered, and one thread from every lowered repeat is raised. In this action certain threads become crossed between the two sheds, causing these threads to be subjected to greater strain than the rest.

The background shed is always obtained by threading on background harnesses. These may be hung on *dräll* pulleys, contramarch cords, or a dobby machine may be used.

Fig. 77 A shows a simple pattern for damask towels, with B giving a detail of the pattern in a five-harness satin weave.

There are always as many background harnesses as there are

Fig. 78. Damask weaving with weaving sword. (Society of Friends of Handwork School.)

warp ends in the basic repeat. The threading is consecutive, with one thread in each dent. In order to permit the pattern shed to be open within the eyes of the background heddles, the heddle eyes should be particularly long (Fig. 16 and Fig. 75). In the tie-up plan both the harnesses to be lowered and those to be raised for each weft are indicated. The treadle draft for the background is always in consecutive order.

Fig. 76 illustrates how the shed is formed for the first weft shot in Fig. 77 B. First, the pattern shed is raised by one of the methods to be described below. The first ground treadle is then depressed, so that the first harness raises every fifth thread from the lower part of the shed, and the second harness lowers every fifth thread from the upper part of the shed (cf. Fig. 76). The first, third and fourth pattern squares will then be warp-faced and the second, weft-faced. The other four treadles are then depressed in turn before a new pattern shed is formed.

Fig. 77 C shows a pattern in eight-harness satin with four threads in each square. It is worthy of note that a cut can be obtained in this weave, which is certainly an advantage, for the pattern is clearly defined. In a five-harness satin damask a cut cannot be produced. However, it is of little significance, since this weave has shorter floats. The clearly defined cut is also of minor importance, if the pattern is of free design, rather than composed of straight lines.

Fig. 77 D–J show tie-up plans for the more common damask weaves. Provided that each pattern square comprises four threads and these are threaded in the same pattern heddles, a cut can be produced with four-harness twill and cross twill (D and E). With six threads in each pattern square and the tie-up plan G, there will be a cut when weaving an irregular satin. Cross twill on six harnesses will produce a cut in one direction only, i.e., along the warp (H). In eight-harness satins the cut can be obtained if the pattern square comprises eight threads, or four threads, as in C, and the tie-up plan is made according to J.

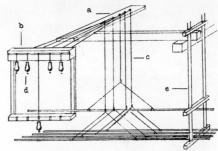

Fig. 79. Draw loom arrangement.

Damask weaving with a weaving sword. An advantage of using a weaving sword (*skälblad*) is that it is possible to weave damask on an ordinary loom, developing any pattern whatsoever without the necessity of resorting to considering the repeat division. However, if the loom is too short from front to back, it will be necessary to extend its length in order to place the warp beam as far back as possible (see photograph, Fig. 78). Weaving according to this system is naturally a very slow process, but it can be made easier, if the pattern is such that it can be wholly or partially picked up on heddle sticks using half heddles.

In setting up the pattern in Fig. 77 A with four-harness cross twill as the basic weave, the threading is in consecutive order on four harnesses using heddles with two-inch eyes. The harnesses are tied to the treadles according to E, using *dräll* pulleys (Fig. 24) for the upper tie-up.

Dräll pulleys can be used for all weaves with an even number of harnesses, but not for those requiring an odd number, such as five-harness satin. One harness is tied to each treadle, and as it is depressed, the opposite harness is raised by the upper tie-up. The harnesses which are to remain in central position are then adjusted by the weaver with the shuttle and one hand.

Pattern A of Fig. 77 can be picked up on five heddle sticks. It will simplify the process to weave this design on the reverse side of the material, so that only the threads needed for the pattern are picked up. Every shaded square on the pattern diagram represents four warp threads. The threads represented by the shaded square

133

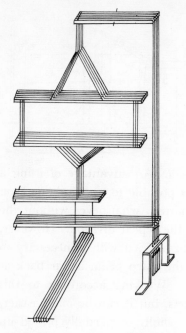

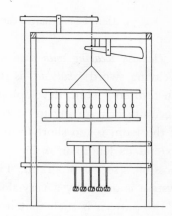

Fig. 80. Contramarch for damask loom.   Fig. 81. Contramarch with contra lamm.

in the center of each pattern stripe (see harness One in threading draft) are now picked up on a stick in front of the reed, this stick then being replaced by one in back of the heddles. A string heddle is looped around each group of pattern threads and is tied, thus resembling a half heddle. The loop ends of the so-called half heddle are slipped through a heddle stick (Fig. 78). The warp threads corresponding to the second, third and fourth harnesses are picked up in the same way. Only one heddle stick, the fifth, is required for the border stripes, corresponding to the sixth harness in the threading draft.

To weave the first row of the pattern, the first, fourth and fifth pattern heddle sticks are lifted and a four-inch wide sword is inserted in back of the heddles in the shed which is formed. The sword is turned on edge and the background treadles are depressed in turn. Following four weft shots, the sword is withdrawn, and the third

134

and fifth pattern heddle sticks are lifted for the second pattern row. In this way the pattern heddle sticks are lifted in different combinations according to the requirements of the design being woven.

Damask weaving on a draw loom. A draw loom is considerably longer than an ordinary loom. This type of loom has a group of 10 to 30 pattern harnesses, which are raised with the aid of draw cords, and a group of background harnesses, which are either tied to *dräll* pulleys or to a contra-march arrangement.

The *draw device* consists of a set of pulleys, a frame and draw cords (Fig. 79). The pulley holder *a* rests on cross bars on the upper part of the loom, while the frame *b* is attached to the front of the loom. A draw cord *c* is tied to every pattern harness. It is then carried over a pulley in the pulley-holder, through a hole in the upper area of the frame, and finally, is provided with a handle *d*. When the pattern harnesses are at rest position, the handles are at the upper area of the frame. The harnesses are raised when the cords are pulled down and the handles are fastened to hooks in the lower area of the frame. To steady the pattern harnesses, they rest on two side frames *e*. There should be a space of fourteen inches between the pattern harnesses and the background harnesses.

A damask pattern which is to be woven on a draw loom must be graphed with a limited repeat warpwise. If the loom has thirty pattern harnesses, the repeat may contain thirty different pattern rows. Fig. 77 A, which has six different pattern rows, can be woven with six pattern harnesses, or with eleven harnesses, if drafted with pointed threading. In the weft, however, the pattern repeat can be very large, for there is an almost unlimited number of combinations in which the harnesses can be raised.

The warp is threaded on the pattern harnesses first, using the long pattern heddles described on page 29. Several threads are drawn through one heddle, the number depending upon the weave and set of the warp. Then the warp is threaded on the background harnesses using long-eyed heddles, with one thread in each heddle.

The pattern harnesses should rest in a lowered position when the shed is closed. In other words, the harnesses should be the same distance *below* the central position in a closed shed as they are *above* when they are raised. The lower heddle stick should be weighted, or a small weight may be attached to each pattern heddle.

If the loom does not have a contramarch arrangement, the background harnesses can be tied to *dräll* pulleys (see weaving with weaving sword).

The *contramarch* arrangement in a damask loom functions in the same way as it does in an ordinary contramarch loom (see p. 243). In addition, however, there must be a device for returning the harnesses to the central position between each treadling. Two harnesses only are tied to each treadle. The harness to be raised is tied from the corresponding long lamm, and the one to be lowered from the corresponding short lamm (Fig. 80). The other harnesses are to remain in central position (cf. Fig. 75). For this purpose, draw cords, weights, springs, or contra-lamms may be used, of which weights or contra-lamms are to be preferred.

Fig. 80 illustrates how weights are attached to a contramarch arrangement for damask weaving. The cords from the top lamms pass through holes at the extremities of the long lamms. Knots are made on the cords, which then pass through another set of holes in a wooden frame resting on the floor. Finally, weights are attached to the various cords in such a way that the weights rest on the floor when the harnesses are in central position.

In Fig. 81, a contramarch with a *contra-lamm* may be seen. The contra-lamm, which is triangular in shape, is movably attached to an axle near the top of the loom. The cord that connects the top lamm to the harness passes through the triangular point of the contra-lamm. When the harness is lowered, the point is pulled down by a knot on the cord, and when the treadle is released, the harness returns to its central position by the weight of the contra-lamm. The movement of the lamm is restricted by a board above the pointed end.

When damask is woven on a draw loom it is usually done with

Fig. 82. Damask weaving with draw harness device. (Society of Friends of Handwork.)

Damask napkin. (Swedish Handcrafts Society.)

the reverse side up, as this reduces the number of pattern harnesses to be raised. For every shaded square in the first row of the pattern diagram, the corresponding draw cord is pulled down, causing the harnesses to rise. The background treadles are depressed in turn for as many weft shots as the design is to contain. Continuing in this manner, the cords for the succeeding pattern rows are drawn down, according to the design.

Damask weaving on a draw-harness loom. A draw-harness loom differs from a draw loom in that the pattern heddles of the former are not hung on harnesses but are tied directly to the draw-harness cords (Fig. 82).

The *draw-harness* will contain as many cords as there are pattern heddles. The cords pass from the heddles through a draw-harness board or a reed, then over the loom, through still another reed, and are attached to a beam above the weaver. The lower parts of the draw-harness heddles are weighted.

The same rules apply for the background harnesses as were discussed in the text on the draw loom.

138

The pattern is inserted in the draw-harness after the warp is set up. For every row on the pattern diagram, loops are threaded under the cords which correspond to the shaded squares. These loops resemble the half heddles described in the section on weaving with a sword. The loops for each pattern row are grouped together and tied with a cord.

A damask pattern, which is woven on a draw-harness loom, need not have a limited repeat in the width. The pattern inserted in the draw-harness system, can vary from one selvedge to the other. For every pattern row in the warp, as shown in a pattern diagram, the loop and cord are inserted. Thus, a repeat consisting of thirty pattern rows will include thirty cords with loops in the draw-harness.

There is, of course, nothing to prevent dividing the width into repeats. Each draw cord is then tied so that it will control several heddles, i.e., one in every repeat. Dividing into repeats simplifies the inserting and weaving considerably, but at the same time, it limits the variety of patterns.

To weave, a cord with loops is pulled down and a rod inserted over the lowered draw-harness cords. The rod is fitted into a frame in front of the weaver. The lowered draw-harness cords will cause the corresponding draw-harness heddles to rise, and in this way the pattern shed is formed. If it is too heavy an operation to pull all of the cords down simultaneously with the rod, they may be taken in groups and attached to hooks.

The background treadles are depressed and the weft shots woven in as previously described. The weaving is continued by pulling down the next cord with loops, and when all cords have been drawn down and the wefts woven in, the entire repeat will have been completed. The cords are then returned to their original positions and the weaving continued.

Damask weaving on a Jacquard loom. A Jacquard loom which is used for handweaving damask, consists of a Jacquard machine and a draw-harness device, as well as background harnesses (Fig. 83. See also p. 251, Jacquard loom).

A Jacquard-woven *damask* should not be confused with the
ordinary Jacquard *weave*, Fig. 74, which is woven without background harnesses. In the Jacquard machine, the hooks lift the
draw-harness cords, and the cards serve the same purpose as the
previously discussed cords and loops. The background harnesses
are usually tied to a contra-march arrangement, or to a dobby.

The width of the pattern repeat depends upon the number of
hooks or needles in the Jacquard. The most usual numbers of
hooks or needles are 200, 400 and 600. The number of cards in
the chain depends upon the length of the pattern repeat and may
be greater or less than the number of hooks. The number of hooks

140

can also be divided so that a certain number are used for a border and the remainder for the main panel of a cloth.

The pattern is drawn on squared paper like an ordinary damask pattern, and the cards are perforated in accordance with the pattern.

To weave with a Jacquard machine and contramarch, the Jacquard treadle is first depressed and fastened down to the floor. The background treadles are then depressed in turn (Fig. 83). When one pattern row has been woven, the Jacquard treadle is released, whereupon a new card acts on the machine, and a new pattern shed forms when the treadle is again depressed. Weaving then continues by depressing the background treadles.

When the background treadles are tied to a dobby, two treadles are used, i.e., a Jacquard treadle and a treadle for the dobby. The dobby must be of a type which both raises and lowers the harnesses (p. 253), and must also have a device for returning the harnesses

Damask table cloth (C. Widlund.)

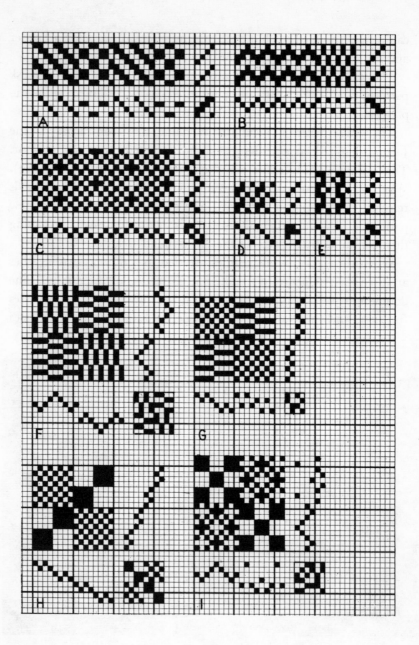

Fig. 84. Combined striped or checked weaves of different structures.

142

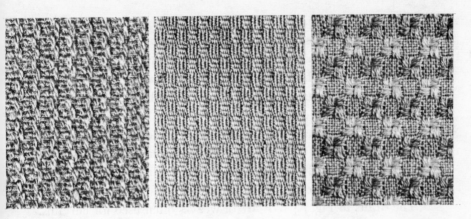

Fabrics using weave patterns Fig. 84 E, F and H.

to their central position. For this purpose, springs or weights are used similar to the contramarch.

Combined striped or checked weaves of different structures. Two or more weaves of different construction may be combined to produce a simple pattern, or to give a particular effect.

Cotton fabric in tabby and weft-faced rep. Cotton 16/2; reed 15 dents per inch, 2 ends in a dent.

A combination often used for a suiting fabric is a four-harness Batavia and a basket weave 2/2 (Fig. 84 A). The weaves go well together and the warp threads have the same number of intersecting points, producing the same amount of warp take-up. This is of considerable importance in all striped combinations, unless the stripes are very narrow.

Another point to take into consideration in a striped combination is to make certain that there is a cut between the stripes, so that they stand out clearly. If a sharply defined cut cannot be obtained, the weaves should be drafted with the best possible pattern division.

The drafts in Fig. 84 B–E are of weaves often used for curtains.

Cloth in M's and O's, warp cotton 30/2. Weft linen no. 30. Reed: 25 dents per inch, 2 ends in a dent. (Society of Friends of Handwork.)

In checked combinations the number of intersecting points are of less significance, since the weaves alternate and consequently even out as the weaving progresses. However, combining a large tabby square with a large twill square would result in an unsatisfactory fabric, as there would be less take-up in the twill, causing it to shrink more than the tabby.

Fig. 84 G, which is a combination of tabby and weft rep 4/4, is called "Poor Man's Huck," or "M's and O's." Here it is given in its simplest form, but it is often woven in checks of varying sizes according to two-block *dräll* patterns.

Fig. 84 H and I are very good combinations for table cloths, etc.

SIMPLIFIED *DRÄLL* (OVERSHOT), MONK'S BELT AND *UPPHÄMTA* WEAVES

In these weaves, a background of warp and weft, usually in tabby, is combined with weft floats alternating on the right and reverse sides of the fabric and producing the actual pattern.

Simplified dräll or overshot

In simplified *dräll* a pattern, that in satin weave requires ten to twenty harnesses, can be woven on only four harnesses (Fig. 85). Simplified *dräll* is produced in several variations, of which Dalecarlian *dräll* and Jämtland *dräll* (also called crackle weave) are the most common. It should perhaps be mentioned here that both Dalecarlia and Jämtland are Swedish provinces. Another simplified *dräll* pattern is known as half *dräll*.

To avoid too long floats in the pattern wefts, certain warp threads are used to bind them down. In a two-block half *dräll* these binding threads occur at regular intervals, e.g., every fifth thread is a binding thread, as in Fig. 85 A and B. The Jämtland *dräll*, or crackle weave, always contains closely set binding threads. One in every four threads serves as a binding thread. The Dalecarlian *dräll*, on the other hand, has binding threads only in instances where the pattern is made up of large squares like those in pattern D. In

145

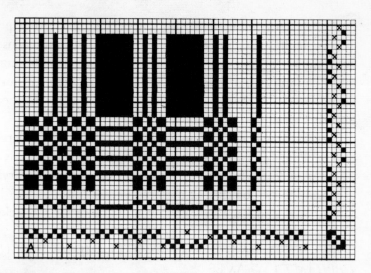

1 square in short draft
represents 10 threads.

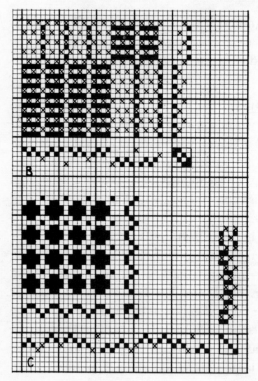

1 square in short draft
represents 4 threads.

Fig. 85¹. Simplified *dräll*
patterns.

146

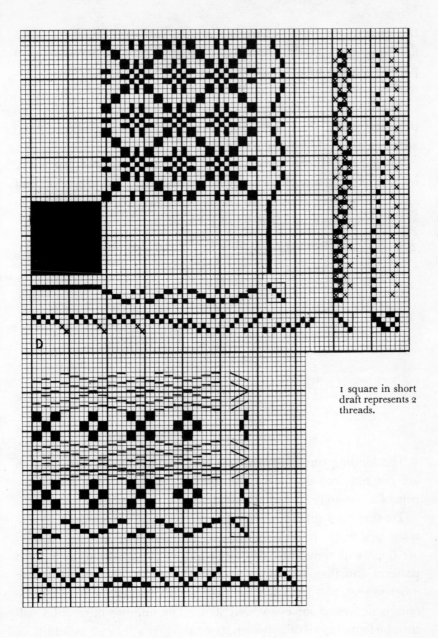

1 square in short
draft represents 2
threads.

Fig. 85². Pattern in simplified *dräll*.

147

this pattern the large square is threaded with two binding threads following six threads. As a rule, binding threads are used in a pattern square which is larger than one-eighth of an inch, if the material is planned for a table cloth.

The draft of a simplified *dräll* can be constructed directly from the short draft, since there are definite rules for threading, tie-up and treadling (cf. *dräll*, p. 122).

Threading: every pattern block is threaded on two harnesses, with careful attention being given to threading alternately on odd and even harnesses. Patterns consisting of two, three or four blocks are threaded on four harnesses as follows:

No. of Blocks	Block	Harnesses
2	I	1–2
	II	3–4
3	I	1–2
	II	3–2
	III	3–4 or 1–4
4	I	1–2
	II	3–2
	III	3–4
	IV	1–4

The binding threads are always threaded on the harnesses which are not required by the block threads, and continue to follow the rule of alternately threading on odd and even harnesses.

Tie-up: two different systems may be used. According to one system, a single harness is tied to each treadle, and two treadles are depressed simultaneously according to the treadling draft. All patterns can then be woven with four treadles. According to the other system, two harnesses are tied to each treadle and one treadle only is depressed for every weft shot. The number of treadles will then be four-six; in other words, two tabby treadles and, in addition, one treadle for each block.

148

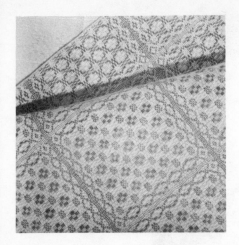

Table cloth in Dalecarlian *dräll*.

Table cloth in Dalecarlian *dräll*.

149

Table cloth from
province of Väster-
götland, Sweden.

Treadling draft: simplified *dräll* is woven using one pattern and
one tabby treadle alternately. For the pattern wefts, the same block
treadle is depressed until the pattern block is woven to the desired
height. Another block treadle is then used according to the treadling
draft.

In weaving the tabby wefts, the left and right tabby treadles are
depressed alternately. When weaving with two shuttles, the left-
hand treadle is always depressed when the shuttle is at the left side,
and the right-hand treadle is depressed when the shuttle is at the
right.

Fig. 85 A is a two-block pattern for a towel. B is a detail of a
simplified *dräll* with drafts.

150

Aprons in different techniques: left, apron in honeycomb; below, one in rosepath; two upper, monk's belt. (Swedish Handcrafts Society.)

Fig. 85 C is a *dräll* pattern in three blocks drafted as a Jämtland *dräll* (crackle weave). The threading here is somewhat more complicated than it is for other simplified *drälls*. This is partly due to the fact that two blocks may be pattern forming simultaneously. Notice the first and second blocks in the left-hand row of the short draft tie-up in C.

In addition to the general rules mentioned above, Jämtland *dräll* requires one thread in four as a binding thread. If a pattern block ends with a binding thread, the next block must begin with a binding thread. The threading will then be pointed, which is characteristic of Jämtland *dräll*. Fig. 85 C is an illustration. The threading is as follows, with the binding threads indicated by underscoring: block II—3, 2, 3, 4; block I twice—3, 2, 1, 2, 3, 2, 1, 2; block II—3, 2, 3, 4; block III—1, 4, 3, 4 repeat. Jämtland

151

Cotton fabric. Cotton 30/2 for background and unbleached double-spooled cotton for pattern. Reed: 20 dents per inch, 2 ends in a dent.

Weaving from Dalecarlia, Sweden.

dräll patterns are frequently based on a four-harness Batavia motif, i.e., comprising four blocks of which two and two form patterns simultaneously.

Patterns in Dalecarlian *dräll* generally contain four blocks.

The pattern given in Fig. 85 D shows tie-up and treadling drafts for either four or six treadles. The former is more suitable for looms without lamms, while the latter is better for looms supplied with lamms.

Fig. 85 E is a striped pattern in which the borders indicated by short dashes are woven on the block treadles without tabby shots between them.

Another pattern can be worked out according to the short draft in F, and a similar treadling draft.

In Dalecarlian *dräll* there are also instances where two blocks form a pattern at the same time. When threading a pattern like

Fig. 86. Monk's belt from Halland
Province.

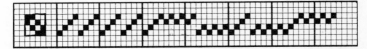

Fig. 87. One repeat of threading and tie-up drafts in Fig. 86. Linen no. 20
for background. Three strands of rose cotton 30/2 and blue. For the
pattern double strands of linen no. 20. Reed: 20 dents per inch, 2 threads
in a dent.

this, there should always be an odd number of threads in each
square, with only one binding thread at a time. Binding threads
must also be used in the transition between the two blocks which
are simultaneously forming the pattern.

Table cloths in simplified *dräll* are usually woven with a cotton
warp and linen weft in all white. However, a superior fabric is
obtained when both warp and weft are woven of linen. Colored
cloths may be satisfactorily woven in all-cotton.

153

Fig. 88. *Upphämta* weave from Halland Province. (Handcrafts Society at Halmstad.)

Simplified *dräll* is also used for other fabrics, such as upholsteries, bedspreads and rugs.

Monk's belt

Monk's belt and similar weaves (Figs. 86 and 87) differ from the *dräll* weaves discussed previously, since the pattern is usually divided into horizontal stripes with plain backgrounds between, and the fabrics are woven in many colors.

Among the monk's belt patterns is the characteristic eight-pointed star with the upright lines between. Individual stars are sometimes woven in, in the background areas between the pattern bands.

All of these patterns comprise two blocks only, and have no binding threads. The two blocks are threaded on two sets of harnesses. The two block harnesses and the two tabby harnesses are then tied down to block and tabby treadles (Fig. 87). One or two background wefts are woven between each pattern weft.

154

Threading draft for background harnesses for weaving *Upphämta* with sword or draw device. (One square represents one warp thread.)

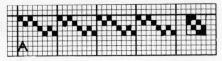

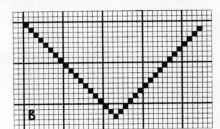

Threading draft for pattern harnesses in weaving with draw device. (One square represents four warp threads.)

Fig. 89.

Upphämta weaves

These weaves may be relatively simple in pattern, as in Fig. 88, or may be very richly decorated with narrow and wide bands between which there are often laid-in designs (Fig. 90). In any event, *upphämta* cannot be woven as an ordinary harness weave, but requires either a weaving sword or a loom supplied with a draw device or a draw-harness arrangement.

One type of *upphämta*, which is often called Småland weave (named for the province of Smaland, Sweden), has continuous all-over patterns which are woven with background harnesses and pattern harnesses tied to treadles.

Upphämta weaving with a weaving sword. The use of a weaving sword permits complete freedom to vary a design. The warp is beamed on an ordinary loom and is threaded through long-eyed (2 inch to $2\frac{1}{2}$ inch) heddles according to the threading draft (Fig. 89 A). The harnesses are tied to the first and fourth treadles, so that the threads will be divided into groups of four, each group then corresponding to a square in the pattern diagram, and to the second and third treadles, which are used for the tabby background.

Weaving is done with the *reverse side up.* When the pattern shed is to be picked up, the first or fourth treadle is depressed. Using a

155

sword, the pattern is picked up according to the design. For every shaded square, four threads are raised over the sword. The four outer selvedge threads on either side should have no pattern. When the pattern shed has been picked up on the sword, it is transferred to a two and one-half inch wide weaving sword inserted behind the heddles. This sword is raised on edge for the pattern weft, after which it is moved back toward the warp beam, while one or two background wefts are shuttled. Each pattern square generally contains three to four pattern wefts.

If the pattern rows are symmetrical weftwise, the pattern sheds are kept on narrow sticks at the warp beam. When the middle of a pattern stripe has been reached, these sticks are brought forward in turn and are replaced by the weaving sword. If any pattern sheds recur constantly, they are picked up on heddle sticks with half heddles in the same manner as has been described.

Upphämta on a draw loom. On a draw loom the warp is first threaded on pattern harnesses and then on background harnesses. The number of pattern harnesses depends upon the number of different rows of pattern squares in the warp repeat. Threading is usually pointed, with four threads in each heddle (Fig. 89 B). The threading on the background harnesses and the treadle tie-up of these are the same as when weaving with a sword.

Although the width of the pattern repeat is limited by a certain number of pattern harnesses, the height of the pattern repeat can be unlimited, since the pattern harnesses may be drawn in different combinations.

This weaving is also done on the wrong side. The pattern harnesses corresponding to the shaded squares in the diagram are drawn up. One or two background wefts are woven in between the pattern wefts, and may be shuttled in even though the pattern shed is raised. Changes in color often take place in the borders and laid-in designs, so that several shuttles as well as "butterflies" or hand bobbins are used (Fig. 91).

Småland weave (Fig. 92). This type of *upphämta* can be woven on

156

Fig. 90. *Upphämta* weaving from the province of Blekinge, Sweden. (Society of Friends of Handwork.)

157

Fig. 91. *Upphämta* weaving on a draw loom. (Society of Friends of Handwork School.)

an ordinary loom, which is not too short. There are usually four to six pattern harnesses, depending upon the number of different weft pattern rows. In the warp, the pattern can be varied by means of the special threading.

The two tabby harnesses are placed nearest the warp beam and the warp threaded with one thread in each heddle, alternately on the first and second harnesses. On the pattern harnesses four threads are threaded for every row of shaded squares in the threading draft. When all of the squares in a row are shaded, the same threads are threaded through heddles on the first, second, third and fourth harnesses. If the squares are blank, the threads are drawn forward between the heddles. Ordinary heddles or those with two-inch long eyes may be used for the background harnesses, while heddles with four-inch long eyes are used for the pattern harnesses. The background and pattern harnesses should be about twelve inches apart.

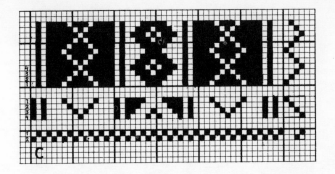

Fig. 92. Pattern for a Småland weave.

Because the same threads are threaded through the heddles of several harnesses, a shed can be produced only by lowering the harnesses, not by raising them. It is therefore advisable to replace the regular pulleys with elastic tape or springs.

In all of the *upphämta* weaves mentioned here, the weft has been used to produce patterns. However, patterns can also be woven in vertical stripes by using special warp threads. The pattern warp would then require an extra warp beam. If the stripes are narrow, that portion of the warp can be wound on spools and weighted. In contrast to the previously described weaves, this type is called "vertical *upphämta*."

The patterned fabrics seen in Figs. 93 and 94 are not woven as *upphämta* weaves, but as one-group harness weaves on ordinary looms, or preferably on contramarch or dobby looms. (See p. 242.) Fig. 94 gives the pattern diagram for the upholstery fabric which is seen in the center of Fig. 93. It can be woven with twenty harnesses and eighteen treadles or on a dobby loom with twenty harnesses and a card chain comprising sixty-four cards. The pattern in Fig. 95 is used when perforating the cards. Fig. 96 is an illustration of a cotton fabric woven with the pattern in the warp. For a pattern of this kind a separate pattern warp is wound on an additional warp beam.

Upholstery with
pattern in weft.
(Swedish Hand-
crafts.)

Patterned weave. (Swedish Handcrafts
Society.)

Patterned weave. (Swedish Handcrafts
Society.)

Cotton fabric.

Fig. 93. Upholstery fabrics. (Swedish Handcrafts.)

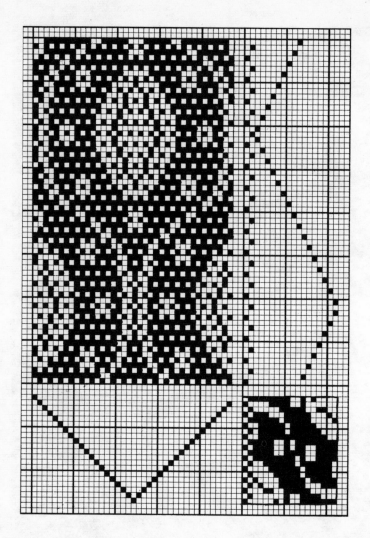

Fig. 94. Pattern diagram for fabric in center of Fig. 93.

BACKED FABRICS

The backed fabrics form a transition between single weaves and double weaves. In backed fabrics one thread system is single and the other is double. Warp-backed fabrics have, therefore, a face warp and a reverse warp with a common weft. Weft-backed fabrics have one warp and a system of face and reverse wefts.

The yarn on the *reverse* side is usually of a poorer quality than

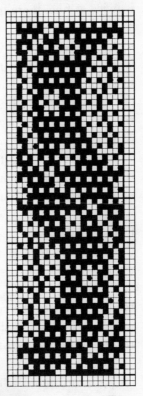

Fig. 95. Perforated pattern for Fig. 94.

Fig. 96. Cotton fabric with pattern in the warp.

163

that used on the *face* side. In instances where the weight of the yarn is the same, the number of threads on the face and reverse sides are generally the same, also. On the other hand, if the face side yarn is twice as fine, there may be twice as many threads on the face side as on the reverse.

A *warp-backed* twill weave is shown in Fig. 97 A. The face warp is indicated by lines on the odd warp rows, and the weave is filled in according to *a*. The binding points of the reverse weave should not be visible on the face side and, therefore, the reverse warp thread is raised between two raised face warp threads. This rise is indicated by a circle.

The warp is either threaded consecutively or with the face warp threads on harnesses one through four and the reverse warp threads on harnesses five through eight.

Fig. 97 B shows a warp-backed broken reversed Batavia on the face side with one reverse warp thread following two face warp threads. The reverse thread is raised once in *every other* repeat of the face weave.

A *weft-backed* twill is seen in Fig. 97 C. In order to conceal the binding point of the reverse weft, it is placed in between two face weft floats. Fig. D shows a weft-backed basket weave with one reverse weft following two face wefts.

Backed fabrics are used for machine woven suitings, as well as for patterned fabrics like blankets and rugs.

Fig. 97 E shows weave C in a checked combination suitable for a rug. It is to be woven with two different colors in the weft according to the design at the left of the pattern diagram. The first dark weft is a face weft in the left-hand check and a reverse weft in the right-hand check. The next weft shot is a light one, and is a reverse weft in the left-hand check and a face weft in the right. In this way one check will be dark and the other light. After weaving eleven wefts, two light weft shots follow, whereupon the left-hand check will become light and the right check dark.

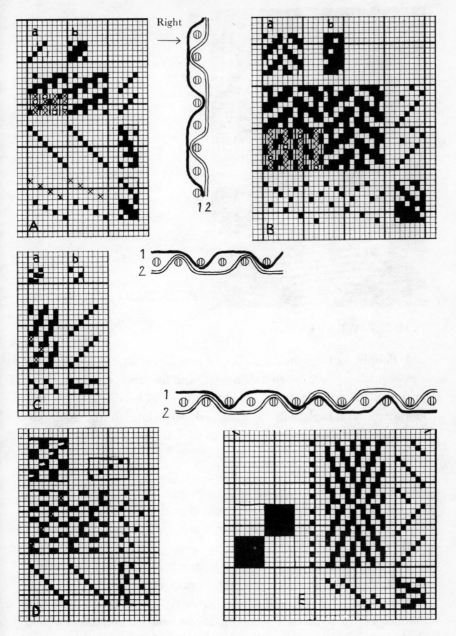

Fig. 97. Drafts for backed fabrics.

Detail of weave E.

DOUBLE WEAVES

A double weave fabric consists of two layers of cloth, one face weave made up of a·warp and a weft, and one reverse weave comprising a warp and a weft. Double weaves to be discussed in the following paragraph will be classified according to the methods employed in joining the two layers to each other.

Tube weaves

In these fabrics both layers are joined at the edges by alternately weaving the same weft in the face warp and then in the reverse warp.

The pattern diagram for a tube weave in tabby may be seen in Fig. 98 A. There should be an odd number of threads in the warp, so that both selvedges will bind correctly. To ascertain that the number of warp threads for both layers will be suitable for the cloth desired, a diagram of the weave is drawn up.

Fig. 98 A is constructed as follows:

1. The face layer in tabby is marked according to *a*, and the reverse layer according to *b*.

2. To distinguish the face layer from the reverse layer, every *odd* row of squares in the warp and weft repeat is marked with a line in the center. (Cf. Fig. 101 A.)

3. The face weave *a* is marked with shaded squares on the lines (center) which cross each other. For the first face weft, the first face warp thread is lowered (shaded square) and the second is raised. For the second face weft, the first face warp thread is raised and the second is lowered (shaded). (Cf. Fig. 101 A.)

4. The reverse layer *b* is ×-marked on the blank squares. For the first reverse weft, the first reverse warp thread is raised and the second is lowered (×-marked). For the second reverse weft, the first reverse warp thread is lowered (×-marked) and the second is raised.

5. When the face wefts are being woven, the entire reverse warp threads are lowered. This is marked with two vertical black lines on every reverse thread. Thus the repeat 4 × 4 appears as shown on the graph. The squares are ×-marked, shaded or marked with two vertical lines signifying lowered warp threads, and blank squares with one vertical line or crossed lines.

6. Outside of the repeat, every lowered warp thread is shaded. Thus, eleven warp and twelve weft threads are shown. The draft is worked out in the usual manner as seen in Fig. 38. It is obvious that a tabby weave in two layers requires twice as many harnesses and treadles as a single tabby weave does.

Double width fabrics

These fabrics are interwoven at one edge only, and will open out to twice their width, when removed from the loom. In this way a wide blanket, for example, can be woven on a narrow loom.

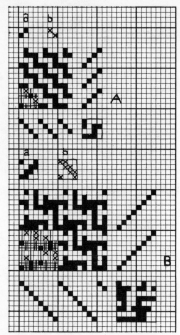

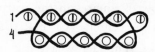

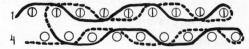

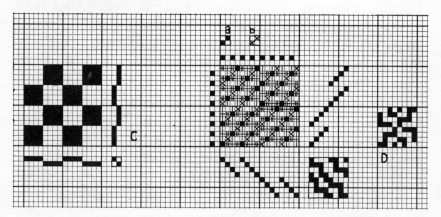

Fig. 98. Pattern diagram for double weaves.

The first and second wefts are shuttled in in the face warp, and the third and fourth in the reverse warp, continuing with two shots in the face warp, and two in the reverse, etc.

The pattern diagram in Fig. 98 B is a four-harness Batavia. To distinguish the face layer from the reverse layer, every odd row in the warp repeat is marked with a line in the center. In the weft repeat, the first, second, fifth and sixth rows are marked with lines. In order to have a fabric in continuous right diagonals when the material is opened out, the reverse weave is drafted as a left-diagonal twill. At the interwoven edge, the set of the warp ends should be spaced a bit more than for the rest of the warp, to avoid a heavier stripe down the center of the unfolded fabric.

Striped, checked or decorative double weaves

These are generally woven in two differently colored layers and are joined when these layers are interchanged according to the design desired.

Fig. 98.C illustrates a checker-board design at left, with its pattern diagram in tabby weave at right. The design with its short draft indicates how the layers should alternate and which color should form the face-side layer. Every row of squares in the design represents one face and one reverse side thread in the pattern diagram. The design has been drafted in four repeats, but the pattern diagram contains one repeat only.

The 16 × 16 pattern diagram repeat is first divided into quarter sections corresponding to the four checks in the design. The interchange of colors in warp and weft is indicated by a row of squares above and to the left of the pattern diagram.

The lower left check in the design is black. Consequently, the black warp and weft threads should be indicated as the face layer in the corresponding quarter section of the pattern diagram. Therefore, warp and weft threads 1, 3, 5, 7 are marked with center lines for the first eight wefts of this quarter. The upper left check of the design is white, and so the white warp and weft threads become the face layer in the corresponding upper left quarter of the pattern diagram. Thus, warp threads 2, 4, 6, 8 and wefts 10, 12, 14, 16 are marked with center lines in that section. The lower right quarter is similar to the upper left, and the upper right quarter is like that of the lower left.

If we examine the first black warp thread, it weaves as a face thread in the lower left (black) quarter and as a reverse thread in the upper (white) quarter. The next white warp thread weaves as a reverse thread in the lower (black) quarter and as a face thread in the upper (white) quarter, etc. In transition between the quarters there are two face and two reverse warp threads. The weft changes position in the same way as does the warp.

The face tabby weave *a* and the reverse tabby *b* are constructed in the same manner as was described for Fig. 98 A. Compare the diagrams.

The checker-board design can be regarded as a block pattern similar to a *dräll* pattern. The two blocks here are indicated in the short draft. In double weave, two tabby blocks require $2 \times 2 \times 2$, or eight harnesses and treadles. In general, color changes in the pattern take place at the same time as the two layers change places. In this way the colors never mingle. If, however, color changes take place without any change in the position of the two layers, there will be a blending of color in the same way as in simple tabby plaids. This checker-board pattern may be used advantageously for handwoven blankets.

Fig. 98 D shows a double tabby weave in one color with frequent changes in the position of the layers. This weave is found in high quality machine woven suitings. Often the alternate threads are S- and Z-twisted, giving the fabric a tricot-like appearance.

As in the damask and *upphämta* weaves described earlier, double weaves may have more elaborate designs, which are then woven on draw or draw-harness looms. The warp is first threaded on the pattern harnesses, with several threads drawn through each heddle,

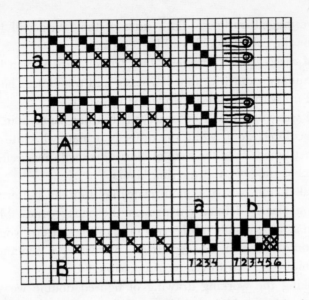

Fig. 99[1]. Threading drafts for background harnesses to be used for double weave with a draw device. B a Threading draft for figured double weave (*Finnväv*) on ordinary loom; *b* on contramarch loom.

e.g., two of each color. The background harnesses are then threaded, using long-eyed heddles, according to either *a*, or *b* of Fig. 99 A. The upper tie-up of the background harnesses consists of two pulleys on each side. The first and second harnesses are attached to one pulley and the third and fourth to the other pulley. One harness is tied to each treadle.

Two light and two dark wefts are woven alternately. For the light wefts, the pattern harnesses which correspond to the dark squares of the pattern are raised, after which the harnesses containing the light threads are lowered in turn. Tabby will then be woven with the light warp and light weft. For the dark wefts the procedure is reversed. In other words, *the pattern harnesses which correspond to the light pattern squares are raised.*

Following this method, the smallest pattern unit will always consist of a square comprising a certain number of warp and weft threads. Two sides of the square will be even, while the other two will have jagged outlines. Both sides of the fabric will be alike, except for the colors, which will be reversed.

Figured double weave (Finnväv). This technique is woven in tabby on an ordinary loom with four harnesses and treadles. The pattern is picked up with the aid of two weaving swords.

In old weavings it will be observed that one layer is in natural black or colored wool, while the other is in natural white wool or unbleached linen. For the sake of clarity, we will here refer to the two layers as the *light* and the *dark* layers.

Figured double weave is non-reversible and the pattern stands out with a clearly defined cut against the background. Should it be woven as a reversible fabric, two sides of the pattern would have jagged contours, as in checked double weave. (In Finland today this technique is often woven as a reversible fabric.)

In making the working drawing of figured double weave, it is important to have the outer threads of the pattern light threads, for then the design will have sharply defined contours.

In the working drawing (Fig. 99 C), the lines of the graph paper itself represent the dark layer. The light layer is drawn in with lines through the centers of the squares. In this way the pattern will automatically be outlined by light warp and weft threads.

The warp is threaded according to Fig. 99 B with the dark threads on the first two harnesses and the light threads on the last two. The harnesses are tied up to pulleys in the usual manner, and one harness is tied to each treadle, according to plan *a*.

Every pair of wefts in the pattern is picked up with the aid of weaving swords (Fig. 99 D and Fig. 100 A). For the light wefts, the third and fourth treadles are depressed, and the dark warp threads are picked up. The dark threads which come within the pattern are lowered, while all of the other dark threads are placed over the sword. When this procedure has been completed, the sword is placed on edge and the second sword inserted in the shed between the *reed* and the *heddles* (sketch B). The first sword is removed, whereupon the opposite treadles are depressed and this sword is

172

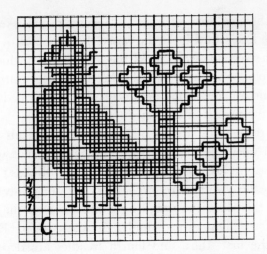

Fig. 99². C Examples of working drawings for double weave (*Finnväv*).

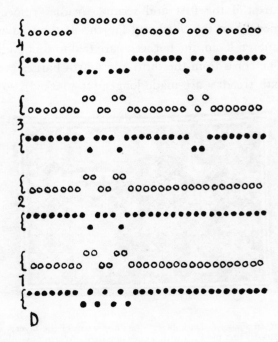

Fig. 99³.

inserted in the shed formed *under* the second sword (sketch C). In this way, the first sword locks the raised dark threads over the light warp and the second sword locks the lowered dark threads under the light warp. For the first light weft shot, the third treadle is depressed, and for the second light weft, the fourth one is depressed, after which the swords are removed.

Now the dark wefts are to be made. The threads are at this point picked up in the light warp. The light threads which come within the pattern are raised and all other light threads are lowered, after which the swords are exchanged as previously described. The swords then lock the raised light threads over the dark warp and the lowered light threads under the dark warp. For the first dark weft, the first, third and fourth treadles are depressed, and for the second dark weft the second, third and fourth treadles are depressed. Thus three treadles are depressed at once. The shed will be clearest if the first and second treadles respectively, are depressed more than the third and fourth. If the weaving is done on a contramarch loom, the harnesses are tied to six treadles according to *b*. The cords from the third and fourth harnesses tied to the fifth and sixth treadles are made longer ($\times$-marked), so that these

Wall hanging in *Finnväv*. Dark layer: tapestry yarn; light layer: unbleached linen 16/3. Reed: 12.5 per inch with 2 ends in a dent. Warps of woolen and linen yarns warped separately.

174

harnesses will be depressed less than the first and second harnesses. The swords are once more removed and weaving continues according to the system for the light wefts.

Figured double weave is very decorative and is used these days for draperies, wall hangings, chasubles, and for many other ornamental purposes.

Stitched double weaves

An interlacing of two weave layers may be carried out by raising certain reverse warp threads and weaving them into the face weft, or by lowering certain face warp threads and weaving them into

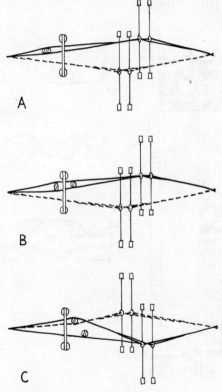

Fig. 100.

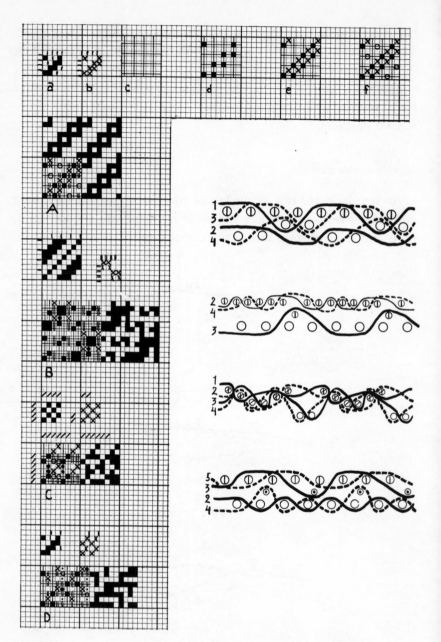

Fig. 101. Stitched double weaves.

the reverse weft (Fig. 101 A, B and C). This can also be done by inserting an additional binding warp between the layers (Fig. 101 D).

These double weaves are used for coat materials of a heavier type, as well as for double woven blankets.

Fig. 101 A shows how a double four-harness Batavia is worked out step by step in the repeat. The face-side draft is indicated by the shaded squares in *a* and the reverse side by the crosses in *b*. Every other warp and weft thread is part of the face-side layer and is indicated by lines through the center of the rows, as seen in *c*. The face-side draft is marked where these lines cross in *d*, and the reverse in the blank squares in *e*. The interlacing of the two weave layers is carried out by raising the reverse warp threads once in every four face wefts. In all other face wefts, the reverse warp threads are lowered. To prevent the reverse thread from showing on the face side of the fabric, it is raised between two raised face warp threads. Moreover, the reverse layer should be placed in relation to the face side layer in such a way that the reverse warp thread is raised before and after the face-side weft in which the stitching occurs. The stitching points are represented by the lines in *a* and by the circles, which indicate rising threads in *f*. Finally, the reverse threads are lowered for face wefts, which are marked by two vertical lines, except where the stitching is indicated. To work out the draft more easily, the remaining repeats are merely drafted with shaded squares. The threading and treadling for this pattern is consecutive, unless it is preferred to thread the face side layer on harnesses one to four and the reverse side layer on harnesses five to eight.

The face-side layer is often made up of a finer warp with twice as many threads as there are in the reverse-side layer. A weave of this type may be seen in Fig. 101 B, with an eight-harness twill on the face side and a basket weave on the reverse. For alternate reverse-side weft shots, a face warp thread is lowered (marked with a dot) between two lowered reverse warp threads. The face-side draft is also indicated by dots with relation to the reverse side, so that the face warp thread is lowered in the wefts before and after the stitching.

Fig. 101 C shows a double weave with double stitching. Both face and reverse weaves are in tabby, and for this reason it will be difficult to conceal the stitching unless both layers are woven of yarn of the same kind and color. In this instance, however, one might select a gray yarn for the face side, while a color effect of two gray and two colored warp threads might be used for the reverse side. The gray warp and weft threads are indicated by diagonal lines at the left and above the pattern diagram. Two face and two reverse warp threads alternate, and two face and two reverse wefts alternate. Stitching takes place by the lowering of the second and third face warp threads in the first and second gray reverse wefts, and by the raising of the first and second gray reverse threads in the second and third face wefts. No stitching takes place between the colored reverse warp threads and the reverse weft shots, since the colored threads are intended to show.

Fig. 101 D shows a double weave with a *binding* warp. The face weave is a four-harness Batavia and the reverse weave is tabby. A binding thread (dotted line) follows two face and two reverse warp threads. Within each repeat it is lowered once for the reverse weft and raised once for the face weft. The binding warp is usually a two-ply cotton in a neutral color.

WEAVE COMPOSITIONS

New weaves may be designed by filling in binding points on squared paper, without following any definite rules. To achieve satisfactory results, however, a basic weave, which is more or less complete in itself, is often used as part of the composition. Likewise, a repeat is marked off, to determine the number of harnesses and treadles the weave will require.

Fig. 102 A shows a four-harness Batavia, in which one binding

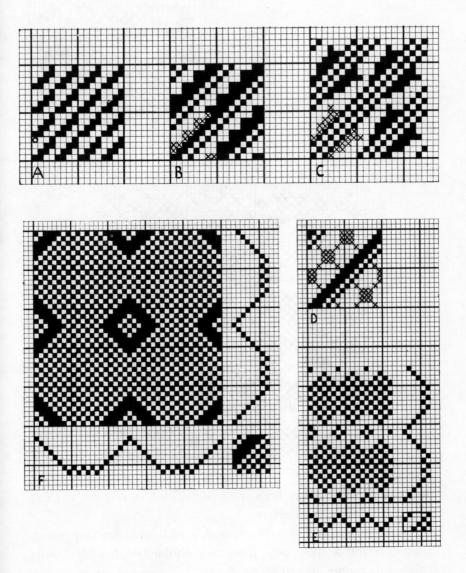

Fig. 102. Weave compositions.

Fig. 102. Weave compositions.

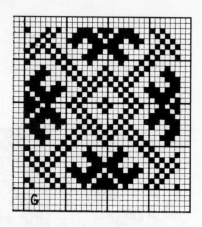

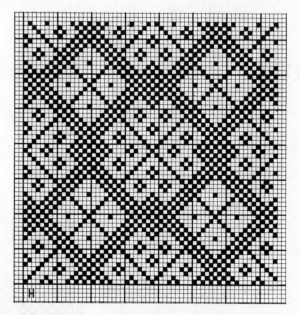

point in the repeat has been omitted (circled in repeat), causing an irregularity in the diagonal.

Figs. B–D are twill weaves containing additional binding points.

Figs. E and F show twill patterns combined with tabby, using pointed threading and treadling drafts.

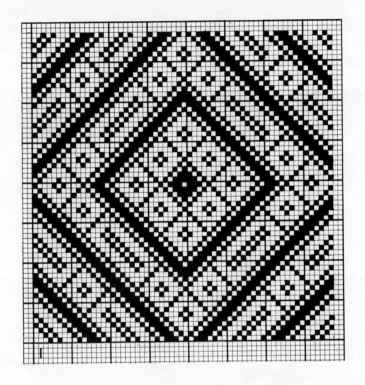

Fig. 102. Weave compositions.

Motif for twill *dräll* from an old weaving book.

Weaves in Fig. 102 G–I are constructed within a repeat of sixteen warp and weft threads, which are further developed by the use of pointed drafts. In G, the same motif appears in the two opposite

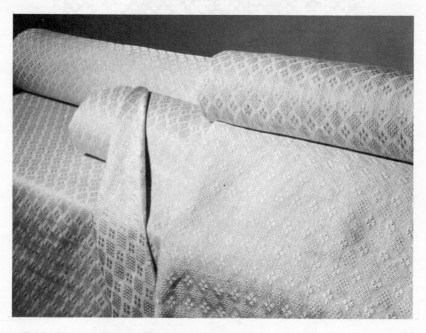

Table cloth in twill *dräll*. (Society of Friends of Handwork.)

Drapery in 16-harness twill *dräll*. (Photo seen from side.)

182

Table cloth in 8-harness twill composition with pattern borders.

corners, while in H, the motifs in the lower left and upper right corners are different.

In Fig. I the pattern repeat is twice as large as those previously described, because of its double pointed draft.

These latter weaves are used chiefly in linen fabrics and are generally called twill *dräll*.

WEAVES IN COLOR EFFECTS

Weaves in which differently colored yarns are combined in the warp and weft to produce small patterns are called "color effects."

Fig. 103 F shows the method of sketching a color effect. The interchange of color in the weft is indicated on a row of squares to the left of pattern *a*, while that of the warp is marked on a row above. The weave repeat is ×'ed in in the lower left-hand corner, and continuing from there, the weft floats are dotted in.

183

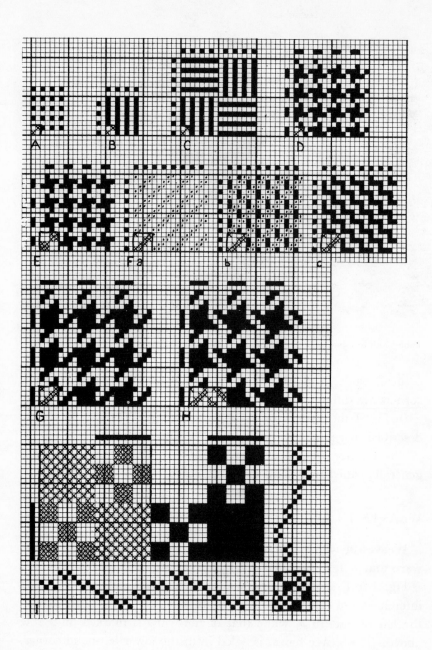

Fig. 103. Color effects.

184

Fabrics in color effects.

When the color effect is to be painted, the following rule is applied: all warp floats on the face side will have the color of the warp shown in *b*, and all weft floats will have the color of the weft as added in *c*.

The most common color effects have special names. Thus, A is called "pepper and salt"; D and E, "pepita"; F, "the little wanderer" or "the racing dog"; G, "cock's footprint" or "shepherd's check," or hound's tooth and I, "rosette pattern."

INTERLOCKED WEAVES

In this group are included those weaves in which the pattern is picked up or interlocked entirely by hand, as well as those in which the pattern is laid in between background wefts.

In the *kilim, rölakan* and tapestry techniques, the pattern is laid in entirely by hand. The weave is weft rep, the fabric consisting of rep surfaces in different colors. These three techniques differ from each other in the manner in which the rep surfaces are held together and in the actual way in which the patterns are formed.

Kilim technique

Kilim is woven by laying in yarns of different colors without interlocking them. This causes slits to be formed in the fabric (Fig. 104 A), which holds together only because the pattern is

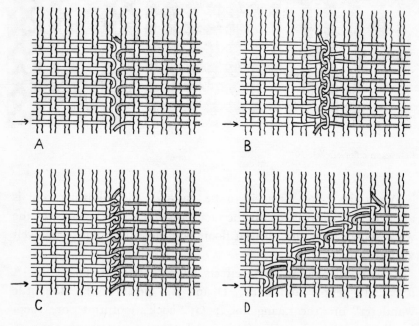

Fig. 104.

developed by its constant movement toward the sides. This is a reversible weave.

Because of its characteristic slits, *kilim* is less compact in appearance than *rölakan*, and is suitable for hangings or can be used in combination with *rölakan* to carry out certain pattern effects (see cross design in Fig. 107).

Rölakan

Rölakan is woven, so far as the interlocking is concerned, in two different ways, i.e., by interlocking the rep areas at each inlay, or by interlocking at alternate inlays.

The former, or double interlocking method, makes the fabric non-reversible and is woven reverse side up. On the right side, the edges of the different areas are even and sharp, while ridges form on the reverse side (see Fig. 104 B). This type of interlocked *rölakan* was commonly used in the old Swedish peasant weavings, particularly in the province of Scania, from which it has received its name of Scanian *rölakan*. Nowadays it is used chiefly for pillow covers.

When alternate inlays are interlocked, the fabric is reversible and the rep surfaces join one another in such a way that the transitions are not so sharply defined (see Fig. 104 C). Since there are no ridges on the reverse side, the surface has a smoother appearance. This method has been used extensively in Norway, and for this reason is called Norwegian *rölakan*. This method of interlocking weft yarns is used in weaving modern *rölakan* rugs.

The smallest unit of a *rölakan* pattern is usually a square comprising two, four, six or eight threads, and as many wefts as are required to complete the square (Fig. 105). However, the pattern can also be woven diagonally (Fig. 106). Thus, one may refer to the first type as squared *rölakan*, and to the second as diagonal *rölakan*. Patterns which are alternately right and left diagonals are called zigzag *rölakan*.

Scanian rölakan. The pattern is drawn up on squared paper, each square representing one or more warp threads. The yarn for the inlays is made into small hand bobbins or "butterflies" (see page 41). The hand bobbins are laid in one of the tabby sheds according to the pattern. The ends of the yarn are fastened back under a couple of warp threads with a half-inch or so left out on the reverse side, which is the side uppermost during weaving.

To interlock the yarn, one hand bobbin is laid in front of the other (Fig. 107).

The laid-in yarns are arranged in even arcs and are beaten *after* reversing the sheds. In this new shed the yarn is interlocked in the same way, but in the opposite direction. When a square has been

Fig. 105. Scanian *rölakan*.

Fig. 106. Diagonal *rölakan.*

completed and the pattern is shifted to the side, a few warp threads can be skipped over on the reverse side of this non-reversible *rölakan.* This facilitates the weaving considerably.

In weaving diagonal patterns, the hand bobbins move with regularity, one warp thread to the side for each inlay. The yarn is fastened and interlocked in exactly the same way as in squared *rölakan.*

Norwegian rölakan. It is more difficult to weave reversible *rölakan* than non-reversible. All weft ends must be so carefully fastened down that they can be cut off at the surface of the fabric. The interlockings must be flat and reversible and the transition of color areas should take place unobtrusively.

Every square in the pattern should contain an even number of warp threads, e.g., two threads. Weaving begins in a definite shed, the one in which the left warp thread is lowered. In this shed the

189

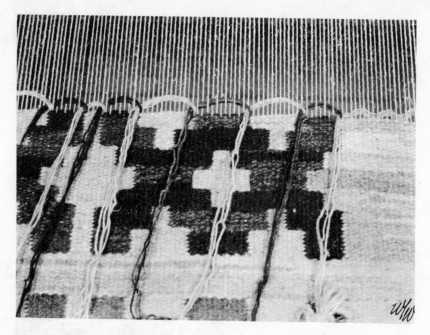

Fig. 107. Interlocking.

inlays are inserted with the yarn ends to the left and under as many warp threads as the pattern calls for. The inlays are not interlocked. After retreadling for the opposite shed, the weft is beaten up.

Before interlocking the weft yarns, all ends are fastened around the raised warp thread on the left side of each color group. If the yarn is double, one is fastened in with a longer end than the other. Interlocking now begins from the right side, and the yarn is laid in even arcs (Fig. 107).

In the next shed the weft is drawn firmly at its left color edge, but is not interlocked (Fig. 108). The interlocking of wefts should be even, smooth and identical on both sides of the fabric.

The number of inlays per square is determined by definite measurement, and allowance is made for a certain amount of packing down of the weft as the weaving proceeds. When a square in the pattern has been completed, the last inlay may be pushed up and the end of the yarn fastened back in the previous shed (Fig. 109). When the pattern requires that an inlay be moved to the side, the yarn is laid in across the previous inlay in the same shed. A new pattern square can likewise be prepared by inserting the yarn end of the new inlay in the same shed as the previous inlay. These pattern changes are always made in the shed in which all of the inlays are drawn firmly (i.e., from the left), and *never* in the shed in which interlocking takes place.

Reversible diagonal *rölakan* is woven in the same way as *kilim*, without interlocking (Fig. 104 D). The difference between these two methods, however, is that in *kilim*, a complete pattern square is woven before the design shifts to the side, while in diagonal *rölakan* the pattern moves two threads to the side every other inlay. Weaving begins in the shed in which the left-hand warp thread is depressed, and every color area must contain an even number of

Fig. 108. Tightening.

191

Fig. 109. Fastening of inlays.

threads. When right and left diagonals appear in the same pattern, the movement to the right takes place in one shed and to the left in the other shed.

Rölakan is frequently woven with several color nuances within the same color area and a particular technique may be employed so that they will blend smoothly. In this instance the bobbins are not laid in in the same direction, but instead, every other bobbin is laid in to the right, and the alternating bobbins are laid in to the left. They are not interlocked, but are shifted to the sides under a varying number of warp threads for each inlay.

192

Rölakan rug "The Red Sea." (Marta Måås-Fjetterstrom AB, designed by M. Richter.)

Rölakan rug. (Swedish Handcrafts Society.)

Tapestry weave

In tapestry weaving, the patterns are much less restricted in form than in *rölakan* and, therefore, greater freedom is permitted in building up one pattern detail after the other without the necessity of weaving across the whole width from selvedge to selvedge for each weft. Tapestry is woven either on a loom with a vertical warp, a so-called Gobelin loom (in French called *haute lisse*), or on a loom with a horizontal, or low warp (*basse lisse*).

A vertical loom consists of two sturdy upright supports, between which are attached a warp beam at the upper end and a cloth beam at the lower. On smaller looms the warp beam is replaced by a cross bar with pegs, to which the warp is stretched. (See photograph "Weaving on a vertical loom.")

194

Weaving on a vertical loom. (Textile Institute, Borås.)

195

The set of the warp is maintained by two yarn chains which are linked into the warp, one at the top and one at the bottom. One shed is obtained simply by inserting a stick in front and in back of every other thread. The second shed is formed by threading half heddles around the warp threads which are behind the stick. The warp threads for this latter shed are drawn forward by means of the heddles.

The weft yarns are wound on tapestry bobbins, which are inserted into the sheds and which also serve to beat the wefts so that a close weft rep weave is obtained. A tapestry is usually woven with the cartoon or design on its side. Thus, the warp will run horizontally and the weft vertically when the tapestry is hung.

The actual weaving techniques vary somewhat in the different *haute lisse* weaves, as may be observed in the French, Flemish and Norwegian (*billedvevnader*) tapestries.

According to the French method, the cartoon or sketch is placed behind the loom and a mirror is attached to the cloth beam, so that the weaver is able to see the right side of the tapestry and compare it to the cartoon. In order to carry out the correct proportions of the cartoon, the outlines of the design are drawn on the warp, as the weaving progresses. When weaving, the tapestry bobbin is held in the right hand, while the left hand is held above at the sheds, alternately drawing out the "stick shed" and the "heddle shed."

It is the rule in French tapestry weaving to lay in the wefts at right angles to the warp. Interlocking of yarns occurs only rarely and the slits which so frequently appear are later sewed together on the wrong side, with button-hole stitching. The colors of the yarns are selected according to the cartoon. Shading of colors is done by means of *hachure*, in other words, by piercing one color into the adjacent color area.

Flemish weave received its Swedish name of *flamskvävnad* when Flemish tapestry weavers introduced this art into Sweden.

The design outlines are traced on tracing cloth, which is then

Detail of Flemish tapestry weave. Warp: linen 30/4 or 18/3. Weft: tapestry wool, 3 strands of each color combination. Set: 11 ends per inch. (Handcrafts Society of Malmöhus Län.)

firmly stretched in back of the warp. No slits occur in Flemish weave, for when two colors meet in a vertical line, the inlays are interlocked around each other or are dovetailed alternately around the same warp thread. *Hachure* is frequently carried out in strongly contrasting colors, and, in addition, contour or outline threads are used. These threads are laid in back and forth following the lines of the built-up contours and, contrary to the rule, are not perpendicular to the warp.

197

Rug: "Wild Strawberries," with borders in *basse lisse* technique. (Marta Måås-Fjetterstrom AB, designed by Barbro Nilsson.)

Both French and Flemish tapestry weaves are non-reversible, since the ends of the wefts are left hanging on the back. Norwegian *billedvev*, on the other hand, is reversible, and all weft ends are woven in. Yarns are interlocked in the same way as they are in Norwegian *rölakan* in places where slits would otherwise occur.

An ordinary loom can function as a *basse lisse* or low warp loom. The beater should be removed and the harnesses replaced by several pairs of short harnesses, each tied to its own pair of treadles. Several persons may work at the loom at the same time, each working independently of the others. The weaving proceeds more rapidly and is not as tiring as at a high warp (*haute lisse*) loom. In all other respects, the weaving is the same.

Within recent years, particularly in France, there has been a revival of tapestry weaving, returning to the original character of the earlier tapestries, where a limited number of colors was used. Furthermore, the artist makes a working drawing from which the weaver works. The design is sketched in with all of the colors to be used indicated by numbers. A tapestry can be woven much more quickly following this system than when the colors are selected according to a cartoon.

Low warp weaving is suitable for tapestries and draperies, as well as for rugs.

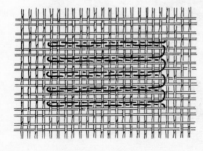 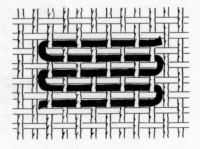

Fig. 110.

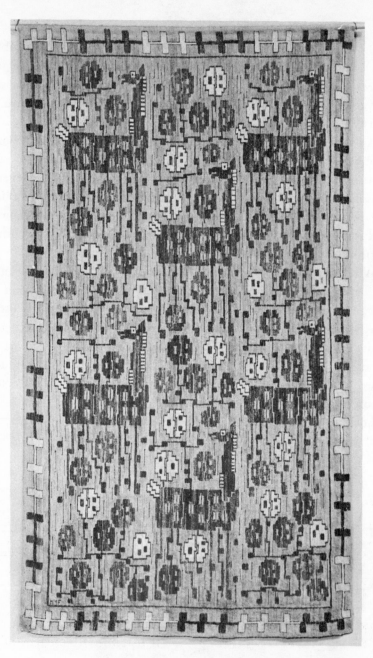

Drapery "Tall Animals," designed by Marta Måås-Fjetterstrom.

Fig. 111. Rag rug with rag inlays.

Simplified rölakan

Rölakan and tapestry techniques can be simplified by shuttling in the background and laying in the pattern areas. One variation is known as the H.V. technique. This technique receives its name from the *Handarbetets Vänner,* or the Friends of Handwork School of Sweden. H.V. technique is woven with a background of close rep weft, with the pattern woven with two inlays followed by two background wefts (Fig. 110, diagram at left). This technique has been used a great deal for linen upholstery fabrics and for pillow covers.

Märta Måås-Fjetterström, a famous Swedish weaver, used another variation. According to this method, the background is woven as an open tabby weave in linen, with inlays in wool. One inlay and one shuttled background weft alternates (Fig. 110, diagram at right). This technique is used for table mats and runners and for draperies.

Fig. 112. Cloth with inlays in *krabbasnår* and borders in *dukagång*. Warp: linen 20/3. Weft: wool no. 6 and inlays of tapestry wool. Reed: 15 dents per inch, 1 end in a dent.

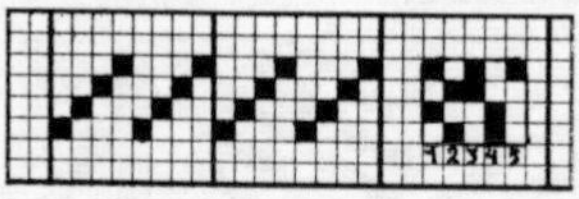

Fig. 115.

Fig. 113. Wall hanging with borders in *halvkrabba*.

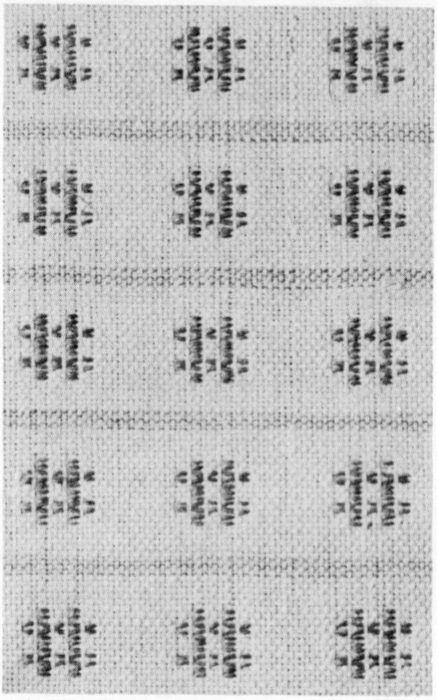

Fig. 114. Runner with *dukagång* patterns.

202

The draperies are made with the woven length as the width of the fabric when hung. Other fabrics, such as curtains, may have inlaid designs worked out in the same way.

Rag rugs may have patterns using inlays or *slarvtjäll*. Pieces of rags are laid in on top of the last woven-in rag weft. Short ends of the pieces are allowed to extend out on either side of the inlay (Fig. 111).

Inlays on rag rugs can also be arranged to show on both sides of the rug. The rags for the inlays should then be cut wide enough so that they can be folded around the rag weft.

Krabbasnår, Halvkrabba, and Dukagång (Swedish terms)

In these three techniques the background weave is usually weft rep. The patterns are laid in in special sheds between the background wefts.

The *krabbasnår* pattern is diagonal in character, with the inlays inserted over one or more threads. The shed for each pattern inlay is picked up by hand (Fig. 112).

Halvkrabba patterns are based on squares. The inlays usually float over two threads, under two, over two, etc., in one square. In the next square the floats go over the *opposite* threads (Fig. 113).

Patterns in *dukagång* are characterized by vertical stripes. These are formed because the inlays always float over the same warp threads and are tied down at regular intervals, e.g., with one binding thread following a float over three warp threads (Fig. 112).

The three techniques are often used in the same piece of weaving, and the threading would then be according to the draft in Fig. 115. In the tie-up plan, the first and second treadles are intended for the background wefts, the third and fourth treadles for the *halvkrabba* inlays and the fifth for the *dukagång* inlays with the weft floats over three threads and under one binding thread. The *krabbasnår* pattern is picked up in a closed shed, i.e., without depressing a treadle.

These techniques are woven *wrong side up* and individual bobbins

Soumak technique. Detail of hanging from Skog.

are used for each figure in the design. The weft ends are fastened by laying them back under a warp thread, leaving about $\frac{3}{8}$ inch ends hanging on the back. A certain number of background wefts are shuttled in between the inlays. The number of wefts should be determined by the build up of the inlays, so that the pattern is neither too extended nor too low, e.g., three or four background wefts between each inlay. The number of inlays in each pattern square should also be adjusted so that the design as a whole will appear in its correct proportions.

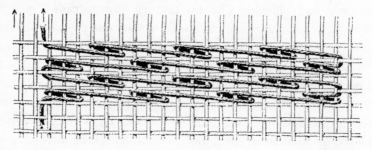

Fig. 116.

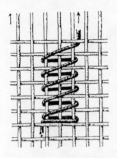

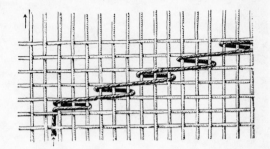

Fig. 117.   Fig. 118.

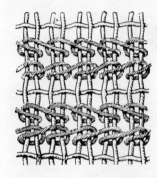

Fig. 119.

If the *dukagång* pattern has a different arrangement of floats and binding threads, for example, with two and one, as in Fig. 114, the shed will have to be picked up on a stick in front of the reed and then be replaced by a weaving sword behind the heddles. The weaving sword is raised on edge when the inlays are to be made, and is moved back toward the yarn beam when the background weft is shuttled in.

These techniques are usually woven with a linen warp and wool singles for the background weft, and with two-ply wool for the inlays. *Dukagång*, however, has been woven very extensively with linen both in the warp and the weft, and with tabby or basket weave as the background weave.

Drapery in *Soumak* technique. (Society of Friends of Handwork.)

Soumak weave (Swedish snärjevävnad)

This technique does not appear among ordinary peasant art weaves in Sweden, but is, however, represented among some Nordic textiles dating from the Middle Ages, the hangings from Överhogdal and Skog.

This inlay is reminiscent of backstitching. In the Skog hanging the pattern weft is laid over nine warp threads, is looped back around the last three, forward again over nine threads, etc. (Fig. 116). When backstitching, the weft yarn is laid in the same direction, but is looped around the three threads previously left free. One tabby shot is thrown between each row of inlay. The background weave is visible between the figures, and each figure is enclosed by a special contour outline. Examples of these contour outlines are shown in Figs. 117 and 118.

In oriental *soumak* rugs, pattern inlays are made in a similar way.

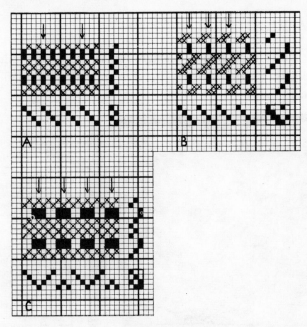

Fig. 120. Pattern diagrams for loop weaves.

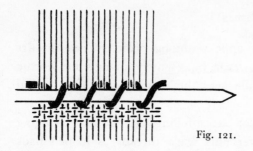

Fig. 121.

The pattern inlay goes over four warp threads, is looped around two of them, over four, etc. (Fig. 119). Returning from the opposite direction, the pattern weft is also laid in the opposite direction, the two inlays giving a chain-like effect. Usually there is one background weft between each pattern inlay or between every other inlay. The *entire* surface of the rug is covered by the inlaid pattern.

PILE FABRICS

A pile fabric consists of a background weave with a pile which completely or partially covers it. The pile itself is made up of cut or uncut loops.

Pillow in loop weave. Warp and background weft: unbleached cotton 30/2. Loop wefts: tapestry wool. Reed: 19 dents per inch, 2 ends in a dent. Draft Fig. 120 C.

Pile fabrics may be classified in three groups according to the method of weaving. The first group includes loop techniques, velvet, etc., in which the pile is formed by drawn up weft or warp threads. The second group comprises the knotted *flossa* and *rya* weaves, and the third, the chenille weaves.

Loop Technique

Loop weaves are woven either as all-white or one-colored fabrics. The pattern is produced by drawing up the wefts into loops in certain areas, leaving flat background areas in between. A heavier yarn is used for the looped wefts than for the flat background wefts. The weave is usually tabby or twill.

Fig. 120 A shows a pattern diagram in which three tabby wefts are woven between each loop weft. The loops are drawn up between every eighth warp thread (see arrows). In diagrams B and C, a separate shed has been provided for the loop wefts.

To weave a loop fabric, first shuttle in a few background wefts, followed by the heavy weft. While the shed remains open, the weft is drawn up between the warp threads and is placed over and under a knitting needle (Fig. 121).

Having completed this procedure, a ground weft is shuttled in, the knitting needle is withdrawn and the weave firmly beaten, after which the other ground wefts are filled in. When the next heavy weft is shuttled in, the process of picking up the loops begins from the opposite side.

If there are to be several colors in the loop fabric, it will be necessary to use hand bobbins, which should be dropped down to the reverse side while the background wefts are shuttled in.

The loop technique is used for bed covers, pillows, rugs and draperies. It is often woven entirely of cotton or with a cotton or linen ground and wool loops.

(Compare loop technique to machine-woven velvet and terry cloth, as well as to bouclé and Wilton rugs.)

Flossa and *rya* techniques are used chiefly for rugs. A *flossa* rug has a close, upright and relatively short pile, while a *rya* has a more spaced and longer pile, which lies flat and covers the background weave. There are also variations of these, and it is a matter of opinion whether they are to be considered as *flossas* with more spaced knots, or as closely knotted *ryas*.

The background weave of a *flossa* rug is usually weft rep. The texture is determined by the number of knots per square decimeter. (One decimeter equals approximately four inches; one square decimeter equals approximately sixteen square inches.)

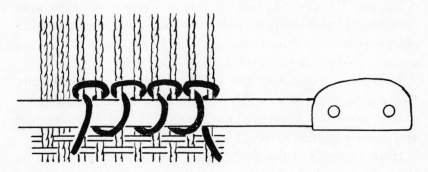

Fig. 122. Knotting over flossa rod.

Fig. 123. Sennah knot and single warp knot.

It is preferable to have the same number of knots on the length as on the width, so that each knot forms a square. A usual texture for Swedish rugs is one having 15 knots × 15 knots = 225 knots per square decimeter. A more spaced texture would have 12 × 12

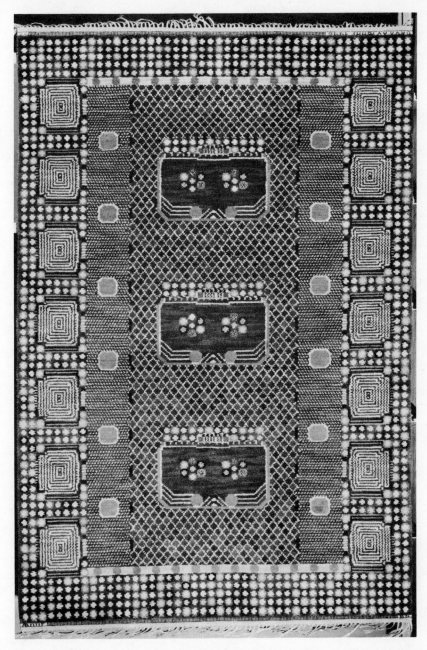

Flossa rug "The Crab." (Marta Måås-Fjetterstrom AB, designed by Barbro Nilsson.)

Rya rug "The Tiger Rug." (**Marta Måås-Fjetterstrom AB,** designed by Barbro Nilsson.)

= 144 knots per square decimeter, and a particularly close texture 25 × 25 = 625 knots per square decimeter. (When classifying oriental rugs, 144 knots per decimeter would be considered as coarse texture, 625 knots as medium fine, 2,025 knots as fine and 4,900–10,000 knots as exceptionally fine texture.)

The design is drawn on graph paper, each square corresponding to one knot. Two warp threads are required for each knot, and in addition, there should be two double warp threads at each selvedge for the extra binding.

The *flossa* yarn is tied over a rod, the size of which is determined by the texture of the rug. The closer the knots are made, the narrower the rod should be.

Examples:

12 rows of knots per 4 inches, 1 row of knots 0.327 inch, 0.316 inch wide rod.

15 rows of knots per 4 inches, 1 row of knots 0.263 inch, 0.275 inch wide rod.

25 rows of knots per 4 inches, 1 row of knots 0.157 inch, 0.157 inch wide rod.

To make a *flossa* rug, begin by weaving in a border of plain rep weft with the same yarn as will be used for the knots. The wefts in this border as well as in the succeeding background, should be laid in small even arcs. This will assist in maintaining the proper width throughout, and avoid the possibility of the edges drawing in.

The rod is now placed on the warp, and knotting begins around the first warp thread following the double selvedge threads (Fig. 122). The hand bobbin is laid under and over the first warp thread, over and under the second thread and under the rod. With the left hand, press down the left side of the knot against the rod, making it taut, then tighten the right side of the knot by pulling the hand bobbin. The yarn should be laid loosely and evenly around the rod, and the knots should not be tightened excessively.

This *flossa* knot is used on Swedish rugs and on most oriental rugs. It is also known as the *rya* knot and the Ghiordes knot. For comparison, the Sennah knot and the single warp knot are shown in Fig. 123. The latter knot is used for particularly fine-textured rugs.

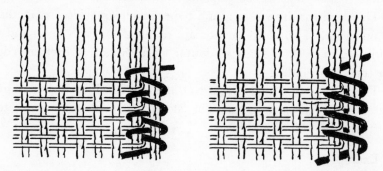

Fig. 124. Flat selvedge binding for *flossa* rug and round selvedge binding for *rya* rug.

When a row of knots has been made, a background weft is woven in. The pile yarn is then cut with a *flossa* knife or with a razor blade attached to a handle. When cutting, the rod should be raised on edge at an angle which will make both ends of the knots equally long. The rug is beaten very firmly, and as the remaining background wefts are woven in, the selvedges are bound, using an extra yarn bobbin (Fig. 124). The background wefts are carefully laid in even arcs and are firmly beaten in a closed shed. With a pile texture of fifteen rows of knots per decimeter, one row of knots with background wefts will be one-fifteenth of a decimeter, and fifteen rows with background wefts will measure one decimeter (see Glossary).

Usually the knots are tied working from left to right. However, some weavers prefer to tie the knots, one row from left to right and the next from right to left. The pile is trimmed as the work proceeds, using a *flossa* scissors, which has curved blades. Bits of yarn and lint which collect on the surface of the rug should be gathered up with the hands, since this brings out the colors more clearly than

Rya rug. Texture 10 × 7. Warp 6/3 linen. Background weft: cowhair yarn. Knots: Walstedt's *rya* wool. Reed: 7–8 dents per inch, 1 end in a dent.

if it is brushed. Before the final row of knots is made, the ends of the yarns used in the bindings at the selvedges and those for the background wefts are fastened in. And finally, a border of rep weft using the same *flossa* pile yarn is woven in. The rug is finished off with an ordinary braided fringe or, better still, with oriental plaiting.

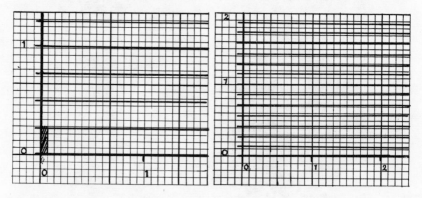

Fig. 125. Dividing of graph paper for *rya* textures 15 × 4 and 10 × 7.

In very old *rya* rugs, such as were used for bed coverings, various background weaves were used, e.g., tabby, rep, twill, *dräll*, and rosepath. However, in modern *rya* rugs, the background weave is, as a rule, weft rep.

In *rya* rugs the texture is characterized by fewer knots per decimeter in length than in width. For example, a *rya* woven 12 knots wide and 6 knots high would equal 72 knots per square decimeter.

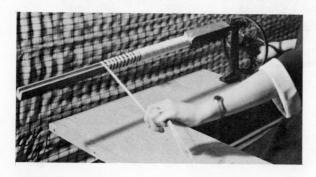

Fig. 126. *Rya* rod.

216

The difference would be even more marked if the rug were woven with 15 knots in width and 4 knots in height, equalling 60 knots per square decimeter, or would be less obvious if it were woven 10 knots × 7 knots = 70 knots per square decimeter. This latter texture is a very satisfactory one, for the yarn ends are well distributed over the surface, giving the rug a fleecy rather than a striped appearance.

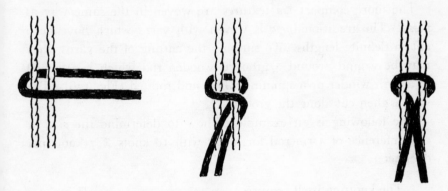

Fig. 127. Tying of *rya* knot using cut yarn.

To secure the correct proportions of the design on the working drawing, it is necessary in some instances to add new lines to the graph paper before the design can be reproduced (Fig. 125). When using 12 knots by 6 knots, every knot is represented by one square in width and two squares in length.

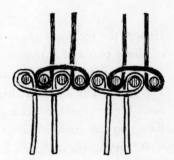

Fig. 128.

Rya knots are not always tied around every pair of warp threads. For example, when using 10 knots by 7 knots, one warp thread is skipped between each knot. The total number of warp ends is then calculated by multiplying the number of squares in the working drawing by three. After the last knot, one warp end is dropped and at each selvedge four ends are added. Thus, the number of squares in the working drawing times 3 minus 1 plus 8 equals the total number of warp ends.

The more compact *rya* textures are woven in the same way as *flossa*. The traditional *rya* is woven with yarns which have been cut in definite lengths. To simplify the cutting of the yarns, they may be wound around a grooved wooden rod which is attached to a yarn winder or a spinning wheel and rotated (Fig. 126). The yarn is then cut along the groove.

The following is an example of how to determine the size or circumference of a *rya* rod for a rug with 10 knots × 7 knots per decimeter.

The knotting itself requires	$\frac{13}{16}$ in.
1 row of knots with background weft requires .	$\frac{9}{16}$ in.
4 in. ÷ 7 rows of knots $\frac{9}{16}$ in.; for the 2 ends of the knot	$1\frac{1}{8}$ in.
1 row of knots should extend over the preceding row of knots at least $\frac{3}{8}$ in.; for both ends, add	$\frac{13}{16}$ in.
	$2\frac{11}{16}$ in.

Hence, the rod for a *rya* of this texture should have a circumference of about two and three-quarters inches.

The cut yarns are tied around the warp threads as illustrated in Fig. 127. The ends of the knots may be uneven so that the pile rows blend smoothly with one another. *Rya* rug designs should be based on *free art compositions* rather than on sharply defined outlines.

When the *rya* is woven for a bed covering, the yarns may be cut

Half flossa rug NUGGET designed by B. Nilsson at M. M.–Fjetterstrom A. B.

twice as long. Each cut piece of yarn is then doubled over and knotted with a loop and two ends forming the pile. The *rya* can also be woven as a reversible rug, and in that case the knots illustrated in Fig. 128 would be used.

A *rya* rug is, in other respects, woven and finished in the same way as *flossa*. A suitable binding at the selvedges is shown in Fig. 124.

Half flossa, relief flossa amd half rya are woven with areas of the flat background showing between the knotted pile. The relief *flossa* rug is one in which the pile is carved or rounded down to the flat surface of the background. *Rya* and *flossa* rugs can also be woven with rods of various widths, obtaining areas of pile at different levels.

Chenille weaves

A chenille rug is twice-woven. First, the chenille itself is woven, after which it is cut in strips. These chenille strips are then used as the weft in the second weave—the actual rug.

In making the chenille, the warp, usually a two-ply cotton, is threaded in tabby. It is drawn through the reed in groups with spacings of from three-fourths to one inch between the groups. For cotton rugs, a heavier cotton yarn is used for the weft, and for woolen rugs, woolen yarn serves as the weft.

If the rug is to have a pattern, the design is sketched on paper in actual size. The paper is then cut in strips, each one corresponding to a chenille weft in the finished rug. These strips are used as the standards of measurement, when weaving the different pattern colors in the first weave. A strip is laid lengthwise along the warp and serves as a guide to indicate how much weft is to be shuttled in for each particular color painted on the strips. When the chenille has been woven and cut in strips, there will be enough weft for more than one rug of the same design.

Ordinary cotton rug warp with tabby threading is used for hand-woven chenille rugs. The chenille strip is laid in the shed and the ends combed so that the pile is divided evenly on both right and reverse sides of the rug. Instead of combing the chenille strips, they can be twisted before weaving in. Between each chenille weft, one background of cotton yarn is generally shuttled in.

Machine-woven chenille and Axminster rugs are woven in the same manner. Upholsteries and draperies may also be woven from special chenille yarns.

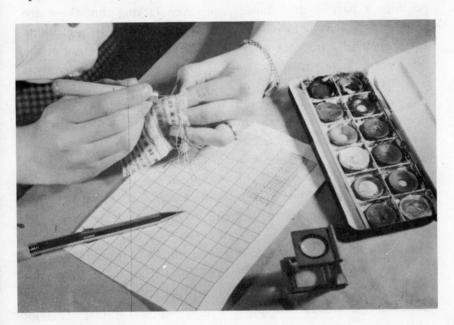

The weave is analyzed.

ANALYSIS OF WEAVES

To analyze the weave of a sample of cloth, it is necessary first, to determine which is the face side, and secondly, to decide which of the thread systems is the warp.

The *face side* is in general easily recognized, since the pattern usually appears more clearly than it does on the reverse, and has a better finish. The face side of sheared woolen fabrics is for the most part cut shorter and more evenly. This becomes more noticeable if the sample is drawn over a finger, first with one side, and then the other, uppermost. Another distinguishing feature in machine-woven woolen twill fabrics is that the diagonal always slants to the right on the face side.

The *warp* is easily distinguished from the weft if the sample contains a part of the selvedge, but even lacking this, there are several ways of recognizing the warp. One of these is to examine the yarn by drawing out a few threads from each direction of the fabric. In single yarns, the warp is found to have a harder twist and if one yarn is ply and the other single, the ply yarn will be the warp. In cases where ply cotton yarn is in one direction and linen or wool yarn is in the other, the cotton yarn is usually the warp (with the exception of half-wool gabardine).

In many fabrics there are space lines in the warp direction, which are caused by the reed. If the reed has been threaded with two threads in a dent, the threads in the warp seem to go in pairs. The warp also appears to be more evenly spaced and the set is usually closer.

For woolen fabrics which have passed through a finishing process, elasticity may be the deciding factor. Stretch an equal amount of the fabric in both directions and it will be found that the weft is more elastic (with the exception of warp rep and a warp rep type of fabric).

When analysing a sample, it should be held face side up with the warp running vertically, as seen in the picture on page 221. A few ends from the left side and from the top of the sample are pulled out. With a coarse needle, or preferably a dissecting needle, the first weft is pushed slightly away from the body of the cloth. Then commencing at the left, observe which warp threads are lowered and raised in this weft. On graph paper fill a shaded square for every *lowered* warp thread and leave a blank square for every *raised* thread. The weave draft should begin at the top row of squares on the graph paper, with the interlacing of the first warp and recorded on the first square to the left. Continue to analyse each succeeding row of wefts and indicate the interlacings on the squares, working down on the graph paper.

It is well to analyze enough warp threads in each weft to make evident a recurrence of the same order, in other words, a repeat.

When the first weft has been examined and recorded on the paper, it is drawn out and the next weft is pushed up and analyzed. This procedure continues until a repeat is completed in the weft also. Analyzing the cloth will proceed more quickly if a soft underlay is placed beneath the squared paper and the shaded squares are pricked with the dissecting needle.

When enough of the weave has been recorded on the graph paper, one repeat is marked off where it is most simply and clearly defined. The repeat is then sketched once more and supplied with drafts, i.e., threading, tie-up and treadling. The drafts also should be the simplest and most practical (cf. p. 52).

If the sample has a very closely set warp, it may be easier to analyze the weft, observing which weft threads lie above and below the various warp threads. In the final recording of the repeat, however, it should be borne in mind that the order is reversed, so that the squares which have been shaded are now blank, and the blank squares, shaded.

Fabrics which are difficult to analyze because they are hard-felted or have a nap may be singed and the fibres scraped off.

Double weaves are dissected in the following manner: A section of the reverse warp and weft threads are drawn out with a needle, so that the face side stands out clearly. This side may now be analyzed. Then a section of the face side warp and weft threads are removed, leaving the reverse threads easily discernible, and this may now be analyzed. In addition, the way in which the two layers are interrelated should also be noted. Do the face and reverse warp threads alternate, or are there, for example, two face threads to one reverse thread? It must then be ascertained how the layers are interlocked. And finally the diagram may be drafted according to the rules concerning double weaves. (Cf. p. 166.)

To analyze fabrics in color effects, it is necessary to record the color transitions at the same time as the weave is dissected. The colors of the warp threads are designated on a row of squares above the pattern and the colors of the weft on a row of squares to the left of it. With the help of the dotted weave pattern and the system of color changes, the diagram of the weave with color effect may be painted. (Cf. p. 184.)

CALCULATIONS OF SET OF WARP AND WEFT

The factors which primarily affect the structure of a fabric are the *yarn* and the *weave*. When the yarn and the weave have been decided upon, the question of a suitable set for the warp and the weft must be determined. A formula is used to calculate the set, which is best explained by the following examples.

Formula: $d - \dfrac{i \times d}{i + r} = s$

Explanation of terms:

d represents the number of yarn diameters per inch (Fig. 129, diagram at top). This number is obtained by winding the yarn to be used around a ruler and counting the number of turns. The threads should lie parallel, as closely as possible without overlapping. For purposes of accuracy, the count should be taken for several inches.

i represents the number of intersections in one repeat of the weave. An intersection is counted when the weft passes between the warp threads from the face to the reverse side of the fabric and vice versa. In the basic weaves as well as in most other weaves, the intersections are counted in the first weft only, as the number is the same in the other wefts (Fig. 129 A, B, and C; cf. Fig. 47).

In weaves with a varying number of intersections, an average is calculated (Fig. 129 D and E).

r represents the number of warp and weft threads in one repeat of the weave.

s is the set, i.e., the number of warp threads per inch in the reed

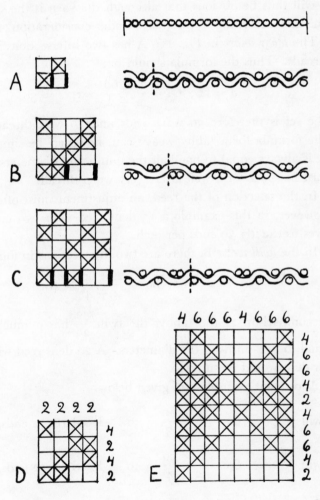

Fig. 129.

and the number of weft threads per inch of woven cloth on the loom. The set is calculated according to the formula above, after the other terms have been established.

The following are examples of the use of the formula in determining the set.

Let us assume that when winding a given yarn around a ruler, there are sixty turns per inch or sixty diameters. For purposes of comparison the same yarn is used in all of the examples to be studied. It will thus be obvious that although the yarn is the same, the set will vary according to the weave under consideration.

The *tabby weave* in Fig. 129 A has two intersections in two warp threads. Thus the formula should be:

$$d = 60; \quad 60 - \frac{2 \times 60}{.2 + .2} = s; \quad s = 30$$

The set is therefore 30 warp ends and 30 weft threads per inch. The formula for a tabby weave can, however, be simplified. The set is always equal to one-half the number of diameters, since there must be space for a weft after every warp thread.

In the selection of the reed, an adjustment must often be made. However, in this example a 15 dent reed with two ends per dent gives us exactly 30 ends per inch.

In the *twill weave* B, there are two intersections in four threads.

$$d = 60; \quad 60 - \frac{2 \times 60}{2 + 4} = 40$$

In comparison to the tabby, the twill $\frac{2}{2}$ has a much closer set, equal to two-thirds of the diameters. A 20 dent reed with two ends per dent would be suitable.

Additional examples are given below.

Twill $\dfrac{2}{1}$ $60 - \dfrac{2 \times 60}{2 + 3} = 36$ Reed 18; 2 ends/dent

Twill $\dfrac{3}{1}$ $60 - \dfrac{2 \times 60}{2 + 4} = 40$ Reed 20; 2 ends/dent

Twill $\dfrac{1\ 2}{1\ 1}$ $60 - \dfrac{4 \times 60}{4 + 5} = 33.3$ Reed 16 or 17; 2 ends/dent

   (Fig. 129 C)

Twill $\dfrac{3}{3}$ $60 - \dfrac{2 \times 60}{2 + 6} = 45$ Reed 22 or 23; 2 ends/dent

Twill $\dfrac{4}{4}$ $60 - \dfrac{2 \times 60}{2 + 8} = 48$ Reed 24; 2 ends/dent

Twill $\dfrac{1\ 3}{1\ 3}$ $60 - \dfrac{4 \times 60}{2 + 8} = 36$ Reed 18; 2 ends/dent

Twill $\dfrac{1\ 1\ 2}{1\ 1\ 2}$ $60 - \dfrac{6 \times 60}{6 + 8} = 25.7$ Reed 12 or 13; 2 ends/dent

The calculations above concern ordinary fabrics in which the set is neither very spaced nor very close and where the same yarn is used in the warp and the weft. This method may be applied as a basis for experimental weaving from which good results will be more easily obtained than without the formula.

When calculating a particularly open fabric like a casement curtain, the set obtained by the formula is reduced 10 to 30%. Similarly, the set may be increased for a fabric of very firm structure, such as an upholstery material.

Allowance must be made for shrinkage when calculating the set to be used for suitings or blankets or any other fabrics which are subject to fulling, felting or other finishing processes. A reduction of the set should be made in proportion to the degree of shrinkage.

If different weights of yarn are used in the same cloth, it is more difficult to find the suitable set. It is, however, advisable to wind the different threads separately around the ruler and then find the average number of diameters per inch. When threads of many different weights are mixed in both the warp and the weft, it may be better to wind them in the same order as they will appear in the weave.

In tabby and basic twill weaves, the warp and weft are equally interlaced, and the set of the warp and weft should be the same. On the other hand, in a *rep fabric* or in other fabrics with a rib structure, one yarn system covers the other (cf. Figs. 41 and 42). To calculate the set of the warp for a warp-faced rep, the number of ends per inch should equal the number of *diameters per inch*. Bear this in mind for the next few pages. There should be only half as many weft threads. The warp threads bend over and under the wefts, which lie straight inside the warp. In a weft-faced rep, there should be twice as many wefts as there are warp ends per inch.

Examples:

> (*a*) warp rep 2/2   diameters 60
>> set: 60 warp ends and 30 weft threads per inch
>
> (*b*) weft rep 2/2   diameters 60
>> set: 30 warp ends and 60 weft threads per inch

When selecting the reed, a particularly close set of warp ends should be sleyed with more than two ends per dent. Thus, a 20 dent reed with three ends per dent would be suitable for the warp rep, while a 15 dent reed with two ends per dent would be satisfactory for the weft rep.

Fabrics in *basket weave* have an equal amount of warp and weft, and therefore, the set is calculated according to the formula.

Example:

> basket weave 2/2   diameters 60

$$60 - \frac{2 \times 60}{2 + 4} = 40$$

> set: 40 warp ends and 40 weft threads per inch
>
> reed, 20 dents, with 2 ends per dent

The set for twill derivatives, especially *pointed twill* and *diamond twill*, is calculated in accordance with the basic weave used. Thus, a goose-eye pattern woven in twill $\frac{2}{2}$ should have the same set in warp and weft as the basic twill.

A *satin weave* is used when a smooth surface and fine set are desired (cf. Fig. 57). It is possible to increase the number of threads per inch in a satin fabric, because the binding points are so scattered that they do not support one another as in a twill. For a warp satin the number of ends are equal to the number of diameters, while the set of the weft is calculated according to the formula. In a weft satin the set is opposite that of a warp satin.

Examples:

(*a*) five-harness satin   diameters 60

$$60 - \frac{2 \times 60}{2 + 5} = 43$$

The warp is set with 60 ends per inch and sleyed in a 20 dent reed with three ends per dent. The weft is woven with 43 threads per inch.

(*b*) five-harness satin   diameters 60

The warp is set at about 43 ends per inch and sleyed in a 20, 21 or 22 dent reed with two ends per dent. The weft is woven with 60 threads per inch. The same rule applies to twill weaves re-arranged in satin order (Fig. 50).

In a *damask* or *dräll* fabric, warp satin is combined with weft satin, and an average number of warp and weft threads per inch is selected.

Example:

(*a*) *dräll* based on 5-harness satin   diameters 60

       warp satin 60 ends; weft satin 43 ends; average 51.5 ends

The warp is set 51 ends per inch and sleyed in a 17 dent reed with three ends per dent. The weft is woven with 51 threads per inch.

Fig. 129 D and E show how an *average number of intersections* is worked out when the threads do not weave alike. The cross twill D has two intersections in the first and third wefts, and four in the second and fourth; the average is 3 intersections. Every warp thread has two intersections. Thus, the average between warp and weft is two and one-half.

$$\text{diameters } 60 \qquad 60 - \frac{2.5 \times 60}{2.5 + 4} = 37$$

If the same yarn is used with 60 diameters per inch, the set of warp and weft will be 37 threads. The warp will be sleyed in a 17 or 18 dent reed with two ends per dent.

The waffle weave in E has an average number of 4.9 intersections and an average number of 9 threads in the warp and weft repeat.

$$\text{diameters } 60 \qquad 60 - \frac{4.9 \times 60}{4.9 + 9} = 38.8 \text{ ends}$$

This gives us 38 or 40 ends per inch, sleyed in a 19 or 20 dent reed with two ends per dent and the same number of wefts.

Many other examples could be given here, but the correct set of a weave is not only a question of theory, but also of experience and personal opinion. It is advisable to use the diameter and intersection formula, and then *try it out* on the loom by weaving a sample before setting up a wide and long warp.

YARN CALCULATION

To calculate the amount of warp and weft yarns required to weave a fabric, certain factors must be established. It will be helpful in working out these calculations, if all pertinent information is recorded on a work sheet. The following is a suggested plan:

WORK SHEET

....

Width: finished width........width on loom........width in reed........

Length: finished length............woven length............warp length........

Yarn: warp yarn .... weft yarn................................

....

....

Set: ends per inch in reed..

wefts per inch on loom..

Reed: dents per inch............................ends per dent........................

Weave: ....

no. of harnesses........................no. of treadles....................

no. of heddles per harness..

Warp arrangement: ....

....

....

Amount of yarn required: warp.......................... weft......................

....

Comments: ....

Explanation of headings:

Finished width is the width of the fabric after it has gone through finishing processes. For cloth which has not been subjected to any finishing, the finished width and the width on the loom are the same.

Width on the loom, or the woven width, is the width of the cloth while still on the loom, with the warp tension released and the stretcher removed.

Width in the reed is the exact width of the warp in the reed. (See also pre-sley width, p. 19.)

Finished length corresponds to finished width.

Woven length corresponds to woven width.

Warp length is the length during warping.

When the finished width and length have been decided upon, the other measurements are calculated with allowance for shrinkage, take-up, etc. For cotton fabrics, towels, table cloths, curtains, etc., a certain amount of shrinkage in laundering is allowed. If this shrinkage is 5% of the width and 3% of the length, the finished width is divided by 0.95 and the finished length by 0.97.

Example: finished width 38 in., width in loom 40 in.

finished length 24¼ yds., woven length 25 yds.

For woolen fabrics and blankets which are to be washed, fulled or napped, the shrinkage varies from 10% to 50%.

The width in the reed should be greater than the woven width, since a certain amount of contraction takes place during weaving. The percentage of width contraction depends partly upon the yarn, the nature of the weave and the set, and partly upon how much the weaver allows the edges to draw in. For normal linen fabrics in tabby, about 5% is estimated, and in twill, about 3%. The amount of width contraction in cotton fabrics is estimated at 7% and in twill 5%. Weaves like waffle weave and honeycomb are calculated with 8% to 10% contraction.

232

Consequently, if the width contraction is 5%, the woven width is divided by 0.95.

Example: woven width $28\frac{1}{2}$ in., width in reed 30 in.

The warp length should also be greater than the woven length, first, because of the take-up or contraction of the length during weaving; and secondly, because the entire warp length cannot be woven. The take-up of the warp is about 2% more than that of the weft. If the weave is firmly beaten, the percentage of take-up is greater than normal, and if the weave is of an open structure, the take-up is less than normal. For fabrics with a warp-faced rep structure, the take-up should be calculated as high as 15%.

The additional length required for tying-in ends and for the thrums (loom waste after maximum amount of weave has been completed) is calculated according to the number of harnesses to be used. For weaves using two to four harnesses, thirty inches should be added, while weaves using five to ten harnesses require forty inches more warp. Weaves of the damask type which are woven on a draw loom need an additional allowance of eighty inches of warp for the thrums.

In addition to these factors, the size of the warping reel must be taken into consideration and the length of the warp may need to be adjusted to the dimensions of the reel (see p. 14). If the warp take-up is 7% and there are four harnesses, the woven length is divided by 0.93, to which result thirty inches are added.

Example: woven length $46\frac{1}{2}$ yds., warp length 50 yds. 30 in.

Warp and weft yarns should indicate the kind, number, bleach or color of the yarns to be used. If several kinds are to be used in the same fabric, the warp yarns may be listed as A, B, C, etc., and the weft yarns as *a*, *b*, *c*, etc.

The number or count of the yarn is based on the length of yarn in one weight unit. In the metric system, the number indicates the number of meters per one gram of yarn.

Example: No. 8 indicates 8 meters per one gram of yarn.

The metric system, which is internationally recognized, is **not** always used. The English system for numbering cotton and linen yarns is commonly used. Cotton yarn No. 1 contains 840 yards per pound and linen yarn No. 1 has 300 yards per pound.

Example: In No. 8 cotton yarn there are 6,720 yds. per lb.

In No. 8 linen yarn there are 2,400 yds. per lb.

Rayon yarn is sometimes counted according to the metric system and sometimes according to the English cotton system.

Yarns of wool are either carded and spun as woolen yarn or are spun as worsted yarn. No. 1 woolen yarn contains 256 yards per pound and No. 1 worsted yarn contains 560 yards per pound.

Example: In No. 8 woolen yarn there are 2,048 yds. per lb.

In No. 8 worsted yarn there are 4,480 yds. per lb.

Silk and artificial silk are numbered according to a French system, which follows an entirely different principle. In this system the number indicates the weight of a unit of length, and is called TD (*titer denier*). To convert to metric count, TD is divided into 9,000.

Example: 1 TD = 9,000 Number Metric; 30 TD = 300 NM.

If a yarn is two or more ply, this is indicated with the number. Cotton yarn 24/2 signifies that there are two No. 24 yarns twisted together. The size of the ply yarn is calculated by dividing the number by the ply. In other words, 24/2 equals No. 12 single. The plying will, however, reduce the length of the yarn somewhat. Therefore, the size of the yarn becomes approximately 6% coarser, a factor to be considered in any calculation.

If the yarn is plied two times, e.g., fish net twine 12/12, the length is considerably reduced. Four groups of three threads are plied. These groups combined form the second plying (12/3 × 4). This makes the size of the yarn about 17% coarser. 12 divided by 12 and reduced 17% equals 0.83. The size of the ply yarn is No. 0.83.

While yarns lose length through plying, they also lose weight through bleaching. It should be borne in mind that the size given refers to the unbleached yarn.

Cotton yarns are obtainable both unbleached and bleached. They lose approximately 6% of their weight in bleaching.

Linen yarns may be obtained unbleached, quarter bleached, half bleached and fully bleached. The loss in weight varies, of course, with each lot of yarn, but there is approximately 10% loss in quarter bleached, 17% in half bleached and 25% in fully bleached linen.

Example: No. 16 unbleached linen yarn, 16 × 300 = 4,800 yds. per lb. (There are 300 yds. per lb. of linen No. 1.)

No. 16 half bleached linen, 4,800 + 17% = 5,616 yds. per lb.

Dyed linen yarns may have been half or fully bleached and, therefore, the loss of weight may vary to a considerable degree. In general, dyed linen yarns lose from 10 to 25% in weight.

Other factors, such as the moisture content of a yarn, may affect the weight of a certain length and width of a yarn. This should be borne in mind when weighing yarn that has been recently washed or dyed.

Set and reed (calculation of set in warp and weft, p. 224).

Weave (see weave construction, p. 49).

Warp and weft arrangement. When a warp consists entirely of one kind of yarn, the warp arrangement is made up of the total number of threads. This is obtained by multiplying the reed width expressed in inches by the number of warp ends per one inch of the reed. If there are varying yarns and colors in the warp, the number of threads of each yarn is noted, and the total of the different numbers should agree with the total number of ends in the warp (see work sheet below).

The total number of weft threads is the number of weft threads per inch multiplied by the woven length expressed in inches. If there are different yarns or colors in the weft, these should be recorded in the same way as for the warp.

Amount of yarn required for warp and weft. The yarn needed is usually computed in pounds. In certain instances it may be more practicable to count in hanks.

First, the number of yards of yarn which is required for the entire warp is determined. This is obtained by multiplying the number of ends in the warp by the warp length. Next, the number of yards required is divided by the number of yards in one pound of yarn.

Example A: warp ends 632, warp length 26 yds.

warp yarn 12/1 half bleached linen

632 × 26 = 16,432 total no. of yds.

(There are 300 yds. in 1 lb. of No. 1 unbleached linen.)

No. 12 × 300 = 3,600 yds. per lb. of unbleached linen.

3,600 yd. + 17% = 4,212 yds. per lb. half bleached linen.

16,432 ÷ 4,212 = 3.9 lbs.

Example B: warp ends 40, warp length 26 yds.

warp yarn 30/2 red cotton.

40 × 26 = 1,040 yds. 30/2 is equivalent to No. 15 single minus 6% for take-up when plied.

(There are 840 yds. in 1 lb. of No. 1 cotton yarn.)

15 × 840 = 12,600 yds. per lb.

12,600 yd. − 6% = 11,844 yds. per lb.

11,844 ÷ 1,040 = 0.088 lb. or approx. $1\frac{1}{2}$ oz.

To calculate the amount of yarn required for the weft, multiply the total number of weft threads by the reed width expressed in yards. Then, as for the warp, divide the number of yards by the number of yards in one pound of yarn.

Example a: Total no. wefts 20,400; reed width $\frac{2}{3}$ yd.

weft yarn 12/1 half bleached linen

20,400 threads × $\frac{2}{3}$ yd. = 13,600 total no. of yds.

13,600 yds. ÷ 4,212 yds. = 3.2 lbs.

236

Example b:　Total no. wefts 1,000; reed width $\frac{2}{3}$ yd.

weft yarn 30/2 red cotton

$1,000 \times \frac{2}{3} = 666\frac{2}{3}$ yds.

$666\frac{2}{3} \div 11,844$ (see warp above) $= 0.056$ lb. (approx. 1 oz.)

If the yarn required is calculated in hanks, the number of yards is divided by the number of yards in one hank.

The following work sheet is based on the figures used above:

WORK SHEET

Dish Towels, 25

Width: finished width $21\frac{3}{4}$ in., woven width $22\frac{7}{8}$ in., reed width 24 in.

Length: finished length 22.7 yds., woven length 23.4 yds., warp length 26 yds.

Yarn:　warp A 12/1 half bleached linen, weft a–A

warp B 30/2 red cotton　　　　　weft b–B

Set:　ends per inch in reed: 28

wefts per inch of cloth on loom: 25

Reed:　dents per inch and ends per dent: 14/2

Weave:　plain weave or tabby

no. of harnesses: 4　　no. of treadles: 2

no. of heddles per harness: 168

Warp arrangement:

A	60 6 4 6 480 6 4 6 60 .	.	.	.	632
B	8 2 2 8　8 2 2 8	.	.	.	40
					672 ends

Weft arrangement:

a   75 6 4 6 634 6 4 6 75 × 25 towels.   .   20,400

b   8 2 2 8   8 2 2 8   × 25 towels .   .   1,000
                                                _____
                                         21,400 wefts

Amount of yarn required: warp A 3.9 lbs., weft *a* 3.2 lbs.

warp B 1½ oz., weft *b* 1 oz.

Comments: The linen tow yarn for the warp should be warp spun. The cotton should be color fast for laundering.

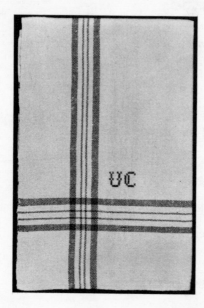

Fig. 142. Dish towel.

238

SPECIAL WEAVING EQUIPMENT

Mechanical sectional warping reel

Bobbin winding, pre-sleying and beaming are time-consuming operations in setting up a warp. Many handweaving studios have, therefore, begun to make use of mechanical equipment to reduce the cost of this work.

Power bobbin winders with eight to ten bobbin holders are used for winding bobbins. These machines are set for either flanged bobbins or cross wound bobbins.

The yarn from these bobbins is warped onto a power sectional warping reel (Fig. 130). This type differs from those described earlier, as it is in horizontal position rather than vertical. At the extreme end of one side, the drum slants outward forming a cone shape.

The warp ends are divided into sections and warping is carried on from as many bobbins as there are ends in a section. The bobbins are placed on a spool rack behind the warping reel and the ends are threaded through a comb, at which point the lease is taken. In order to maintain the exact width of a section, the ends are threaded through an adjustable hinged reed. The ends of the section are tied together and are attached to the drum at the cone-shaped area. The lease is taken and drawn forward to two cords attached to the drum. At the right end of the reel the warp is supplied with a counter, which is set for the desired number of revolutions, according to the length of the warp.

The warping reel is set in motion by depressing a treadle and when the counter indicates the length of the warp, the reel stops automatically. The section of ends is then cut off and tied and the ends for the next section are fastened beside the previous one. The lease is taken for this section, and warping continues until all of the ends have been warped. Because each layer of warp is laid cone-shaped over the previous one, the warp is very even.

Fig. 130. Mechanical sectional warping reel.

The warp is then beamed directly from the drum to the warp beam, which is placed in a stand in front of the drum.

To maintain a firm tension during the beaming process, the warping reel is held in check by a brake. The warp beam moves slightly from side to side, and in this way prevents the threads from working down into the preceding layers. To safeguard the selvedges, flanges are attached to the beam. When the beaming has been completed, the lease appears.

240

A similar method of warping can be carried out using an ordinary warping reel, which is placed in a horizontal position and on which hooks have been screwed into one of the main supports. Each section of warp in turn is tied to a hook. The reel is rotated by hand with the aid of a crank, and the revolutions counted. The threads are wound as on a spool and are *not* cone-shaped as on the previously described machine warping reel. The warp is then ready to be beamed directly, the operation being done by hand.

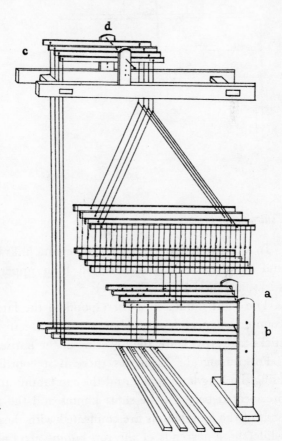

Fig. 131. Contramarch.

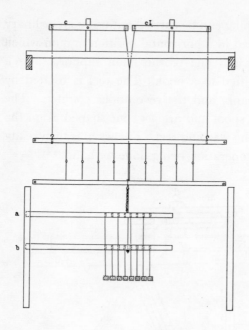

Fig. 132. Contramarch.

Contramarch loom

In a contramarch loom, the connecting links between the treadles and the harnesses, and affecting both upper and lower heddle sticks, are the lamms (Fig. 131).

The short lamms at *a* correspond to the lamms on an ordinary counter-balanced loom. They are tied directly to the lower heddle sticks and provide for the lowering of the harnesses.

For raising the harnesses there is a coordinated arrangement using the long lamms at *b* and the top lamms at *c*. The long lamms are located between the short lamms and the treadles. The outer ends of the long lamms are connected with those of the top lamms, while the inner ends of the top lamms are linked with the upper harness sticks. When a harness is to be lowered, a cord is tied from the corresponding short lamm to the treadle, and when a harness

242

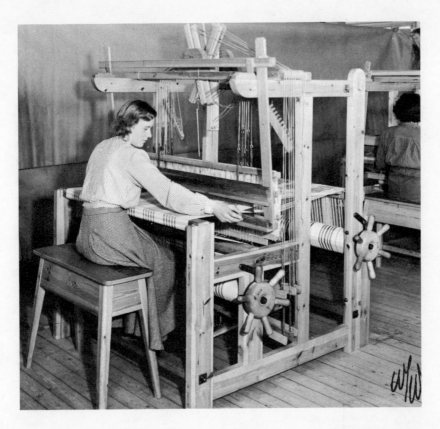

Weaving on contramarch loom with vertical top lamms. (Handcrafts Society at Borås.)

is to be raised, a cord is tied from the corresponding long lamm to the treadle. There should be as many lamms of each type as there are harnesses on the loom. Each harness thus acts independently of the others and the shed will be clear, whether the weave is reversible or non-reversible, and whether it is threaded on an odd or even number of harnesses.

To mount a contramarch on an ordinary loom is as a rule not very satisfactory, since there is not enough room for the axles of the short and long lamms on the side supports. A loom with the contramarch arrangement should, therefore, be taller than an ordinary loom, so that the distance between the axles will be adequate. The top lamms in the upper area of the loom may be mounted in various ways, either horizontally in one or two groups, or vertically.

Contramarch with one group of horizontal top lamms. Fig. 131 illustrates how the top lamms are movably attached at the axle *d*. The weight of long lamms with their connecting treadles rests on the outer arms of the top lamms, while the inner arms are weighted by the short lamms with attaching treadles. Since the weight of the latter is obviously the greater, the axle is placed in such a way that the inner arms of the top lamms are shorter than the outer. Should the lamms still be unbalanced, the outer ends of the long lamms may be weighted.

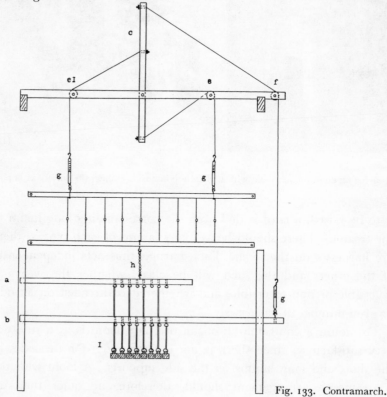

Fig. 133. Contramarch.

One disadvantage, however, of this location of the top lamms is that the harnesses are gradually pulled awry. When the top lamms are in horizontal position, the harnesses are tied to hang in the center of the loom, but when the lamms are set in motion, they describe a semicircle, causing the central point to move sideways and the harnesses to be pulled askew. The sheds are also affected, subjecting the warp to needless strain.

Contramarch with two groups of horizontal top lamms. This arrangement (Fig. 132) is particularly suitable for wide looms. The top lamms at c and c_1 are connected with the lamm at b, which is the same length as the lamm at a. When the lamm at b is lowered, the inner ends of the top lamms are also lowered, while the outer ends raise the harnesses to which they are tied.

The harnesses move straight up and down, producing an excellent shed. The only disadvantage of this type of contramarch is that the long cords running from the top lamms down to the lower lamms pass between the warp threads and may cause a certain amount of wear on them.

Contramarch with vertical top lamms. When the top lamms are placed vertically on the loom, as in Fig. 133, a most satisfactory shed may be produced. However, with this arrangement, the width of the loom should not exceed five feet. The top lamm is movably mounted on an axle in the center of the upper crossbars. One-third of the lamm is below the axle and two-thirds are above. Cords run from the lower part of the lamms over pulleys at e to the right side of the harnesses. From the half-way point of the lamms are cords which pass over the pulleys at e_1 to the left side of the harnesses. Cords also run from the upper part of the top lamms down to the long lamms by way of the pulleys at f.

Because of the equal distribution of the weight a good balance is obtained, and since the cords pass over pulleys the harnesses move easily and always rise and fall vertically.

Tying the contramarch. Every detail of tying the contramarch loom should be carried out with care and precision. During this procedure

Fig. 134. Fly shuttle device. (Textile Institute, Borås.)

246

the top lamms should be locked into position, a device for this purpose being a requisite for every contramarch loom.

The harnesses are tied to the top lamms at a height which brings them in a central position and with the warp running through the middle of the heddle eyes. The harness holders are now removed

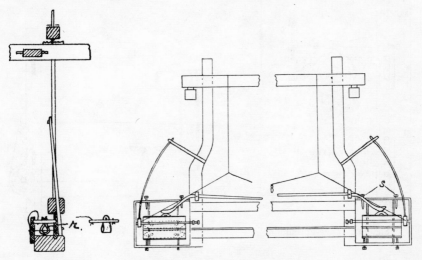

Fig. 135.   Fig. 136. Fly shuttle device with double shuttle boxes.

and the harnesses hang freely. The long and short lamms are tied into horizontal position, i.e., parallel to the floor. If, however, the distance between the long and short lamms is not sufficient for easy movement, the short lamms will have to be tied at a slightly upward angle. For every shaded square in the tie-up plan of the weave to be used, a cord is threaded through the corresponding hole in the short lamm, and for every blank square in the plan, a cord is threaded through the corresponding hole in the long lamm. In all other respects the same rules apply as for an ordinary loom (see page 37).

Tying a contramarch loom need not be time consuming after it has once been done. By using metal adjusters (Fig. 133 *g*) the cords are easily hooked on or unhooked; the chains shown at *h* are the proper length between the lower heddle sticks and the short lamms; and with the special rods on the treadles, seen at *i*, it is a simple matter to attach the previously tied loops to the treadles.

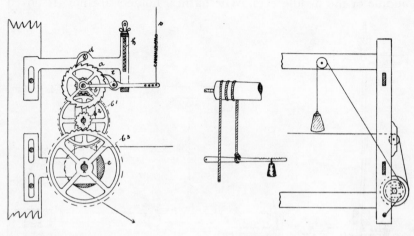

Fig. 137. Take-up motion.   Fig. 138.

Fly shuttle

To weave with a fly shuttle, the shuttle is propelled alternately from a box on one side of the beater through the shed and into a second box on the other side. Fly shuttle weaving is done chiefly on looms where the weaver *stands* at work, such as hand Jacquard looms and certain looms with dobby motion. It is also used to weave very wide fabrics on ordinary looms. The use of a fly shuttle increases the speed of weaving beyond what can be achieved by throwing a shuttle by hand. However, this method is not suited to weaving all types of fabrics. In the first place, there is a greater tension in the weft. Moreover, frequent change of shuttles is not practical. Fly shuttle devices with multiple shuttle boxes are available, but the weft arrangements are then dependent upon the capacity of the shuttles to change.

The beater with the fly shuttle device is extended and equipped with shuttle boxes (Fig. 134) on either side. The lower part of the beater forms a race which slants inward toward the reed. The race continues into, and forms the base of the boxes. There are two sides to the boxes which should be only slightly wider than the shuttle. The rear sides of the boxes should be on a plane with the reed, which should end exactly at the beater swords.

The part that impels the shuttle through the warp is called the picker, and may be made of pressed pigskin. It moves freely on an axle in the upper area of the box, while at its base it glides along a groove on the bottom of the box. A strap is attached from the picker in one box to the picker in the other. This strap is held up by two guide straps suspended from the upper area of the beater. A handle is attached to the strap at its center. To set the shuttle in motion the weaver jerks the handle with sufficient force to cause the shuttle to strike the picker alternately on one side and then the other. (See fly shuttles, p. 248.)

The picker may also be made of a loop of leather attached to a flat piece of wood (Fig. 135). This piece of wood, or lid, to which the leather strap is fastened, slides in grooves on the sides of the box.

A fly shuttle with double shuttle boxes is shown in Fig. 136. The boxes are mounted one above the other, and may be raised or lowered to permit either shuttle to be brought level with the shuttle race. To facilitate movement of the boxes, the picker axles must be placed outside of the boxes. Each time the picker enters a box, it is forced outside by the action of a spring or a bamboo strip.

Automatic take-up

Fly shuttle looms usually have a device known as an automatic take-up, a motion in which the woven cloth and warp automatically move forward as the weaving progresses. The edges of the weave remain in a constant position in relation to the beater, causing the fly shuttle motions to function better and the weft set to be more even.

The take-up motion may be mounted directly on the cloth beam axle, but it is usually placed at the breast beam (Fig. 137). It works in connection with the beater, and at each beat a certain amount of the cloth is drawn forward. A releasing brake on the warp beam lets out a corresponding amount of warp.

In the diagram at the left in Fig. 138 is seen a releasing brake device consisting of a weight bar, a weight and a brake cord. The cord is wound around the warp beam a couple of times, and one end is fastened to the loom and the other to the weight bar. The degree of resistance may be regulated by sliding the weight along the bar. On wide looms it may be necessary to have a brake arrangement at both ends of the warp beam.

Another brake device is shown to the right in Fig. 138. This type is used when the warp beam is placed so low on the loom that there would not be room to install the brake described earlier. The weight in this instance is a sandbag.

The take-up motion consists of a system of cogwheels (Fig. 137). In the illustration these are five in number. The cord s is connected with the beater, which causes an up-and-down movement of the lever arm for each beat. The pawl e is attached to the lever arm, and rotates the ratchet wheel a. From the ratchet wheel the movement is carried to the beam c via the cogwheels b, $b1$, $b2$ and $b3$. A stop pawl d prevents the ratchet wheel from turning backward, while the pawl at e is engaged in taking a fresh hold. By moving the cord along the lever arm, or by changing the cogwheels, the rate at which the cloth is moved forward may be regulated to achieve the desired set of the weft.

The beam at c corresponds, in this case, to the breast beam of the loom. In order to draw the cloth forward, this beam must be round and have a surface which will grip the cloth. In weaving a woolen fabric the beam is covered with sandpaper and for that reason is called a sand beam. Linen weaves require a beam encased in studded metal.

When the cloth leaves the sand beam it is wound on the cloth beam. To rotate the cloth beam, a weight similar to that in Fig. 138 is attached, but in this case the cord is wound several times around the cloth beam and is fastened directly to it. The weight will gradually sink to the floor, and must therefore be rewound at intervals.

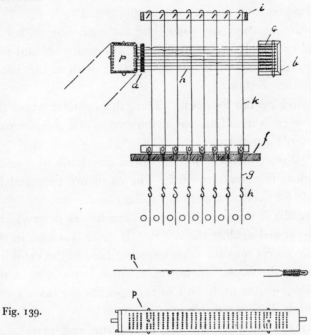

Fig. 139.

Jacquard machine

A loom with a Jacquard machine differs greatly from an ordinary loom. It is made of a strong frame, above which is mounted a Jacquard machine. This machine, by means of a draw-harness, acts upon the heddles with their warp threads.

Only one treadle is used on a hand Jacquard loom, and each time the treadle is depressed, the machine changes to a new shed.

The Jacquard itself consists of a coordinated system of hooks, needles and blades, as well as a card cylinder and card chain.

The hooks are arranged in rows, an example of which may be

seen in Fig. 139 showing a row of eight hooks, *k*. The hooks rest on the bottom board *f*, with the draw-harness cords attached to the upturned lower extremities of the hooks.

The hooks are guided by the needles *n*, which on one side are provided with springs *c*, placed in the spring box *b*. On the other side, the needles protrude through the needle board *a*.

The blades are arranged in rows, one for each line of hooks, and are placed in the blade box or griff *i*. The griff rises and falls vertically when treadling takes place, carrying with it the hooks not affected by the needles.

The card cylinder *p* has four sides. Over this cylinder passes the card chain. For each treadling, the cylinder makes a quarter turn and brings forward a new card.

Every warp thread in the repeat requires one hook and every weft in the repeat requires one card. The cards are prepared by punching a hole for every warp thread to be raised.

When the treadle is released, i.e., raised, the blades descend and the cylinder is pressed against the needle. If there is a hole in the card, the needle enters into the corresponding hole in the cylinder, thus not affecting the hook. If, however, there is no hole in the card, the needle is thrust aside and in turn pushes the hook aside, so that the hook is disengaged from the blade.

When the treadle is depressed the blades rise and carry with them the hooks not affected by the needles. By means of the draw-harness and the heddles, the corresponding warp threads are raised.

As the warp threads are raised only, the warp must at the beginning be in a lowered position. It is drawn down by the heddles, which are weighted.

A hand Jacquard may contain 100, 200, 400, 600, or 800 hooks and needles. A Jacquard of 400 has 8 rows of hooks with 50 hooks in each row, to which are added extra hooks for selvedges. By means of the draw-harnesses, the cords from several repeats may be attached to the same hook. In a Jacquard of 400 hooks and 5 repeats, the warp can thus consist of 2,000 threads.

252

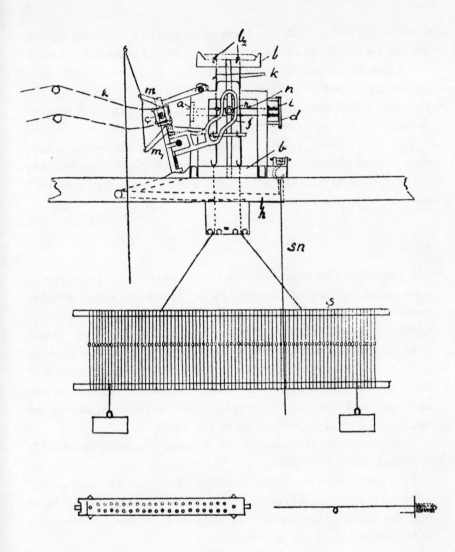

Fig. 140. Dobby machine.

The Jacquard loom has been used chiefly to weave richly patterned fabrics, but upholstery materials of simpler design are also woven on this type of loom. The treadle on this loom is tied up

253

so high that it is necessary to stand while weaving. For this reason, the loom is usually equipped with fly shuttle and automatic take-up.

On damask looms, the Jacquard machine is combined with background harnesses. The pattern shed is obtained by depressing the Jacquard treadle, and while this is lowered, the background treadles are depressed in turn (see damask, p. 140).

This brief discussion of the Jacquard loom will have to suffice, since it is not possible in this book to enter into a detailed explanation of the various harness threadings, the perforating of the cards, etc., used on a Jacquard machine.

Dobby loom

A dobby may be described as an application of the principles of a Jacquard machine to a harness loom. It may be obtained either to raise harnesses, or to both raise and lower harnesses.

Fig. 140 shows a dobby for raising twenty-four harnesses. When weaving with fewer harnesses, a corresponding number of hooks is then eliminated. The hooks are arranged in two rows, of which those in the left-hand row are connected to the left side of the harnesses, and those in the right-hand row to the right side of the harnesses. The lower harness sticks are weighted.

This machine is also operated by depressing a single treadle. It is used to weave multiple-harness fabrics.

The other type of dobby machine, that of both raising and lowering harnesses, differs from the former in that the hooks in one row raise the harnesses, while those in the other, by the action of the lamms, lower the harnesses.

In recent years a loom with a dobby machine has been constructed in Sweden, at which the weaver may sit and weave (Fig. 141).

This is a twenty-harness raising and lowering dobby machine, which is operated by treadling on two treadles alternately. When the right treadle is depressed, the shed opens and the shuttle may

Fig. 141. Dobby machine. (Swedish Handcrafts.)

be thrown by hand or by the fly shuttle mechanism. The shed closes when the left treadle is depressed, and the card chain moves for the next weft.

The cards are of the same type as those used in a number of power looms, and consist of twelve-inch-long wooden staves. The staves are joined in a chain by means of loops and hooks. Twenty holes are bored in each stave, into which wooden pegs can be inserted. This is done following the weave pattern, in accordance with the perforated pattern (see Fig. 95).

The pattern repeat is limited to twenty differently weaving warp threads, while the weft repeat can be much longer and determines the number of card staves in the chain. The card chain passes over a cylinder above which there are twenty steel levers, which are moved by the pegs in the chain. These levers regulate the top lamms, which in turn regulate the harnesses.

This loom can also be used most advantageously for weaves requiring fewer harnesses.

SWEDISH-ENGLISH WEAVING
GLOSSARY AND WORD LIST

ACETAT RAYON GARN—acetate rayon yarn
ADDERA—to add
ÄKTA FÄRGER, HÄRDIGA FÄRG-ÄMNEN—fast colors
ANALYS—analysis
ANALYSERA—to analyze
ANALYSNÅL—dissecting needle, needle for analyzing a fabric
ANBINDNING—stitching, binding of both surfaces of a double-faced fabric
ÄNDLÖS FIBER—filament
ANGIVA—to indicate
ANILIN—aniline
ANORDNING—arrangement
ANPASSNING—adaptation
ANVÄNDA—to use
ANVISNING—instruction
APPARAT—apparatus
APPRETERING—finishing, finish (of a fabric)
APPRETUR—finish (of a fabric)
ARBETSKLÄDER—work clothes
ARBETSRITNING—working drawing
ARVEGODS, SLÄKTKLENOD—heirloom
ÅTTA SKAFT—eight harnesses
ATELJÉ—studio
ATLAS—satin weave
AVBINDA—to stitch
AVBINDETRÅD—binding thread, stitching thread
AVDELNING—division, part, section
AVDRAG—deduction
AVFALL—waste, refuse
AVHASPLA—to reel off
AVIGSIDA—reverse side, wrong side
AVSKÄRA—to cut off
AXEL—axle

BADHANDDUK—bath towel
BÅGE—arc, curve
BÅGNA—to warp, bend, sag
BAKRE STRÄCKBOM—back beam, slab stock
BÄLTE—belt
BAMBU—bamboo
BAND—band, tape, inkle
BANDSKED—band reed, inkle reed

BANDVÄVNING MED KORT—card weaving
BANDVÄVSTOL—band loom, inkle loom
BÅRD—border
BARNFILT—baby blanket
BARNKLÄDER—children's clothes
BÄRNSTENS FÄRGAD—amber colored
BASISKA FÄRGÄMNEN—basic dyes
BASSE-LISSE (FRANSKA)—*basse lisse* (French), low warp, horizontal warp, in tapestry weaving
BASSE-LISSEVÄVNAD—tapestry woven on a low warp loom
BASSE-LISSEVÄVSTOL—low warp loom, horizontal loom
BASTFIBER—bast fiber, raffia fiber
BATAVIABINDNING—Batavia twill
BATIST—batiste
BEARBETNING—adaptation
BEDFORD CORDBINDNING—Bedford cord weave
BEFUKTNING—humidifying
BEHANDLING—treatment, processing
BERÄKNA—to calculate
BEREDA—to prepare
BESKRIVNING—description
BETA—to mordant, to subject to the action of a mordant
BETFÄRGÄMNE—mordant dyestuff
BETMEDEL—mordant
BILD—illustration, picture
BILDVÄVNAD—tapestry weave
BILLEDVEVNAD (NORSKA)—Norwegian tapestry weave
BINDEMÖNSTER—draft, pattern diagram
BINDEPUNKT—binding point
BINDESTRECK—hyphen
BINDEVARP—binding warp
BINDNING—weave, interlacing, binding
BINDNINGSANALYS—analysis of weaves
BINDNINGSKOMPOSITION—weave composition, designing of weaves
BINDNINGSLÄRA—weave construction
BLÅNGARN—tow yarn
BLÅWILLS—denim
BLEKA—to bleach
BLEKNA—to fade

BLEKNING—bleaching
BLIXTRÖLAKAN—zig-zag *rölakan*, laid-in weave
BLOCK—pulley
BLÖTA—to soak
BLUS—blouse
BLY—lead
BOBIN—warp spool
BOBINING—winding of warp spool
BOBINMASKIN—winding reel
BOBINSTÄLLNING—spool rack
BOHUSVÄV—figured double weave, also called *Finnväv* in Swedish
BÖJA SIG—to bend
BOLSTERVAR—ticking
BOMNING—beaming
BOMSPJÄLA—beam stick, rib, lath
BOMULL—cotton
BOMULLSGARN—cotton yarn
BOMULLSLÄRFT—plain cotton fabric
BOMULLSTYG—cotton fabric
BONAD—wall hanging, tapestry
BORDDUK—table cloth
BORDLÖPARE—table runner
BORDVÄVSTOL—table loom
BÖRJA—to begin
BORR—drill
BORRA—to drill, bore, pierce
BORSTA—to brush
BOTTENINSLAG—background weft
BOTTENINSLAG I TVÅSKAFT—tabby weft
BOTTENSKÄL—background shed
BOTTENVÄV—background weave
BRÅKNING—breaking (of flax)
BREDA UT—to spread out, space
BREDD—width
BRICKDUK—tray cloth
BRISTA—to break
BROMS—brake
BROMSTRUMMA—brake drum
BRÖSTBOM—breast beam
BRUK—use
BRUTEN INREDNING—broken draft
BRUTEN KYPERT—broken twill
BRUTEN-OMKASTAD KYPERT—broken and reversed twill
BRUTEN SPETSINREDNING—broken pointed draft
BULT—bolt
BUNDEN—bound, interlaced, tied
BUNDEN ROSENGÅNG—bound rose-path
BUNT—bundle
BYK—washing, laundry

CELLBINDNING—honeycomb weave
CELLULL, RAYONULL—cut rayon

CENTIMETER—equal to 100th of a meter. Abbr. *cm.* (2.54 cm. = 1 inch)
CHAPPESILKE—silk floss
CHEVIOTTYG—serge, 2/2 twill
CORDBINDNING—cord weave
COTTOLINGARN—yarn spun of cotton and linen tow

DALDRÄLL—overshot weave from the province of Dalecarlia, Sweden
DÅLIG—poor
DAMAST—damask weave
DAMASTVÄVSTOL—damask loom
DAMMHANDDUK—dust cloth
DECATERA—a finishing process for woolen or worsted fabrics
DECIMETER—equal to 1/10 meter. Abbr. *dm.* (1 dm. = 3.937 inches)
DEL—part
DELNING—division
DETALJ—detail
DIAGONAL—diagonal
DIAGONALBINDNING—diagonal weave
DIAGONALRÖLAKAN—*rölakan* with diagonal inlay
DIAMANTBINDNING—diamond twill weave
DIVIDERA—to divide
DRAGA—to pull, draw
DRAGA IN STADKANTEN—to draw in at the selvedge
DRAGHÅLLFASTHET—tensile strength
DRAGRUSTNING—draw loom arrangement
DRÄKTTYG—suit fabric
DRÄLL—two to four block weave
DRÄLLDAMAST—four to ten block damask
DRÄLLMÖNSTER—block pattern
DRÄLLTRISSOR—*dräll* pulleys
DRAPERI—drapery, room divider
DROPPDRÄLL—huckaback, spot weave
DUBBELBRED VÄVNAD—double width weave
DUBBELKOPPLADE SKAFT—harnesses tied in pairs
DUBBELSATIN—satin weave with two binding points on every thread in the repeat
DUBBEL SPETSINREDNING—double pointed draft
DUBBEL TVÅSKAFT—double plain weave, double tabby weave
DUBBELTVINNAT GARN—yarn plied two times, double plied
DUBBELVÄVNAD—double weave
DUK—cloth

DUKAGÅNG—inlay technique characterized by vertical stripes

EFFEKTGARN—yarns with textured effect, bouclé, nubby, etc.
EFSINGAR—thrums, warp waste
EFTERBEHANDLING—finishing (of fabric)
EFTERGIVANDE BROMSNING—releasing brake
EFTERSLAG—additional beat made after treadling
EKLÖVSKRANSEN—"oak leaf garland," twill pattern
ENFÄRGAD—monochrome
ENGELSKT GARNNUMRERINGSYSTEM—English yarn count
ENGELSKT KAMGARNSNUMMER—English worsted
ENGELSKT KARDULLGARNSNUMMER—Yorkshire skein
ENKELT GARN, EJ TVINNAT—single yarn
ERHÅLLA—to obtain, receive
ETIKETT, ADRESSLAPP—label
EXCENTER—eccentric

FAKTOR, GEMENSAM—common factor
FÅLL—hem
FÄLL- fleece
FALL (OM TYG)—quality of draping
FALSK, IMITERAD—false, imitated
FÅR—sheep
FÅRAHERDENS RUTA—shepherd's check
FÄRDIG—finished
FÄRDIG VÄV, BEREDD VÄV—finished fabric, processed fabric
FÄRG—color
FÄRGA—to dye
FÄRGÄMNE—dyestuff
FÄRGARE—one who dyes
FÄRGEFFEKT—color effect
FÄRGHÄRDIGHET, FÄRGÄKTHET —color fastness
FÄRGSKIFTNING—changing of color, shading
FÄRGTON—tone of color
FÄSTA—to fasten
FATTA TAG I—to grasp
FATTIG MANS DRÄLL—M's and O's, poor man's huck
FEL—defect, error
FELANDE TRÅDAR—dropped ends (threads)
FEM SKAFT—five harnesses

FIBER—fiber
FIBERFLOR—web
FIBERSTAPEL—staple; quality of a fiber, as fine or long staple
FILT—blanket
FIN—fine
FINNVÄV—figured double weave
FISKBENSMÖNSTER—herringbone twill
FISKEGARN—fish net twine
FJÄDER (AV STÅL)—spring (steel)
FJUN—fuzz, down
FLÄCK—spot
FLÄCKHÄRDIGHET—spot resistant
FLAMFÄRGNING—tie-dyeing, tie-and-dye method
FLAMSKVÄV—Flemish tapestry weave
FLÄNS—flange
FLÄNSRULLAR—spools with flanges at both ends
FLÄTA—braid, plait
FLÄTBINDNING—braided or entwining twill weave
FLOCKA SIG, BLI NOPPIG—to fluff, get fuzzy
FLOCKIG—fluffy, fuzzy
FLOR—gauze, veil
FLOSSA—short pile
FLOSSAKNIV—flossa knife
FLOSSAMATTA—closely knotted, short-pile rug
FLOSSAMATTA I METERVARA, BRED OCH ENFARGAD—broadloom carpeting
FLOSSASAX—flossa scissors
FLOTTERING—float
FLYTTA—to move
FNURRA PÅ TRÅD—kink in the thread
FODERTYG—lining fabric
FÖLJD, I RÄTT—in direct sequcene
FÖRÄNKLAD RÖLAKAN—simplified rölakan, inlay technique
FÖRDJUPNING—depression, hollow
FÖRDRAGSGARDIN, TÄT—window drapery
FÖRDRAGSGARDIN, TUNN—casement curtain
FÖRENKLAD DRÄLL—simplified *dräll*, overshot weave
FÖRKLÄDE—apron
FORMEL—formula
FÖRSKED—pre-sleying reed, beaming reed
FÖRSKEDNING—pre-sleying, preliminary sleying
FÖRSKEDSBREDD—width in pre-sleying reed
FÖRSKJUTEN RIPS—diagonal rep weave

FÖRSTÄRKT VÄVNAD—backed fabric
FÖRSTORAD KYPERT—enlarged twill
FÖRSTORINGSGLAS—magnifying glass
FORTSÄTTA—to continue
FRAMKALLNINGSFÄRGÄMNEN—developing dyes
FRAMKNYTNING—tying on of warp ends
FRAMKNYTNINGSKÄPP—tying rod from cloth beam
FRAMKNYTNINGSÄNDAR—warp ends
FRAMKNYTNINGSVÄV—loom apron
FRAMSKAFT—background harnesses
FRAMTRÄDA—to appear
FRANS—fringe
FRANSA—to fringe
FRANSFLÄTNING—fringe plaiting, braiding
FRANSKNYTNING—fringe tying
FROTTÉVÄV—terry cloth
FUKTIGHETSHALT—moisture content
FYLLNAD—padding, filling
FYLLNADSTRÅD—padding thread
FYRA SKAFT—four harnesses
FYRFLÄTNING—braiding four strands
FYRKANT—square

GAGNEFKRUS—pattern in honeycomb weave from the parish of Gagnef in Dalecarlia, Sweden
GARDIN—curtain
GARDIN, TUNN—glass curtain, casement curtain
GARN—yarn
GARNÅTGÅNG—amount of yarn required
GARNBERÄKNING—yarn calculation
GARNERAD—trimmed
GARNFÄRGAD—yarn-dyed
GARNGROVLEK—weight of yarn, degree of coarseness of yarn
GARNNUMMER—yarn count, yarn number, size of yarn
GARNNUMRERINGSSYSTEM—system of yarn count
GARNSOLV—string heddles
GÅSÖGONBINDNING—goose eye weave
GENOMBROTTSPUNKT—intersecting point
GENOMBRUTEN VÄVNAD—open fabric
GENOMSKÄRNING—cross section
GEMENSAM FAKTOR—common factor
GJUTA—to cast
GJUTEN JÄRNDEL—cast iron part

GLES—open, spaced
GLIDA UPP—give way, slip out
GOBELINPINNE—tapestry bobbin
GOBELINVÄVSTOL—Gobelin-type tapestry loom, vertical loom
GREKISK DRÄLL—Greek huck
GRUNDBINDNING—basic weave
GUMMIRING—elastic band

HACHURE (FRANSKA)—*hachure* (French), hatching, shading (in tapestry weaving)
HÄCKLA—to hackle
HAJOMDRÄLL—overshot pattern from Hajom in the province of Västergötland, Sweden
HAKE—hook
HÅLKRUS—honeycomb weave
HALLANDSDRÄLL—huckaback pattern from the province of Halland, Sweden
HÅLSÖM—hem stitching
HÅLVÄV—open fabric, spaced in the warp or weft or both
HALVBLEKT—semi-bleached
HALVDRÄLL—simplified *dräll* known as half dräll, overshot weave
HALVFLOSSA—half *flossa*, relief *flossa*
HALVKRABBA—inlay technique, pattern based on squares
HALVLINNE—fabric woven with cotton warp and linen weft
HALVRYA—half *rya*, relief *rya*
HALVSKAFT—stick with half heddles
HALVSOLV—half heddle, doup
HAMPA—hemp
HANDTAG—handle
HANDVÄVNING—hand weaving
HANK—loop of twine
HÄRDIG—resistant, fast
HÄRDIGHET MOT FLÄCKAR—spot resistant
HARNESK—draw-harness
HARNESKRUSTNING—draw-harness device
HARNESKSOLV—pattern heddles
HÄRVA—hank, skein
HÄRVEL—reel for winding skeins
HÄRVLING—winding of yarns into skeins
HASPLING—skeining
HÄSTAR, VÄV—horses, rocker arms (on loom)
HAUTE-LISSE (FRANSKA)—*haute lisse* (French), high warp, vertical warp in tapestry weaving)
HÄVSTÅNG—lever, bar
HELBLEKT—fully bleached
HELDRAGEN FIBER—filament

HELLINNE—all linen
HELYLLE—all wool
HJÄLPLINJE—auxiliary line
HJUL—wheel
HÖGERSNODD—right-hand twist, clockwise twist, z-twist
HONUNGSKAKEBINDNING—honeycomb weave
HOPPA ÖVER—to skip, jump
HOPPANDE INREDNING—jumping, irregular draft
HÖRNSTÖTTA—corner post
H.V.-TEKNIK—simplified tapestry weave, a technique from Handarbetets Vänner (Friends of Handwork), Stockholm

IMITERAD—imitated
INDIGO—indigo
INDRAGNING AV VÄVBREDDEN—contraction in width of weaving
INPLOCK—inlay, laid-in
INPLOCKSGARN—inlay yarn
INREDNING—draft
INREDNINGSSKÄL—threading, lease
INSLAG—weft, weft thread, filling, shot, woof
INSLAGSEFFEKT—weft effect
INSLAGSFLOTTERING—weft float
INSLAGSFÖRSTÄRKT VÄVNAD—weft-backed fabric, double weft fabric
INSLAGSHOPPA—weft skip, weft jump
INSLAGSKYPERT—weft-faced twill
INSLAGSORDNING—weft arrangement, weft plan, weft order
INSLAGSRIPS—weft-faced rep
INSLAGSSATIN—weft satin
INSLAGSTÄTHET—closeness of weft
INSTÄLLNING—set, the number of warp threads per inch in the reed and the number of weft threads per inch of woven cloth on the loom
INTVINNINGSPROCENT—percentage of reduction of yarn length when plied
INVÄVNING—contraction of length of warp or weft when weaving, take-up
INVÄVNINGSPROCENT—percentage of contraction

JACQUARDMASKIN—Jacquard machine
JACQUARDVÄVD—woven on a Jacquard loom
JÄMFÖRA—to compare
JÄMNT—evenly
JÄMTLANDSDRÄLL—crackle weave, overshot pattern from the province of Jämtland, Sweden
JÄRNTEN—steel rod
JUSTERA VÄVSTOLEN—to adjust the loom

KAMGARN—worsted yarn
KAMGARNSTYG—worsted fabric
KANTSNÄRJNING—selvedge binding used on *flossa* and *rya* rugs
KÄPPAKLÄ—(provincialism) weaving with sticks in pick-up technique
KÄPPSKÄL—stick shed (in vertical-warp tapestry weaving)
KARDA—to card
KARDGARN—woolen yarn
KASTA SKYTTELN FRAM OCH TILLBAKA—to pass the shuttle back and forth
KASTANJEBRUN—chestnut brown
KASTSKYTTEL—throw shuttle
KAVEL—roller
KEDJA—chain
KELIM—kilim, type of laid-in or tapestry technique
KEMISK TVÄTT—dry cleaning
KIL—wedge
KILOGRAM—kilogram equal to 2.2046 pounds. Abbr. *kg.*
KJOL—skirt
KLÄDNINGSTYG—dress fabric
KLÄMMA—catch, clip; also to squeeze, to press
KLARSKÄRNING AV TYG—close shearing of cloth
KLISTER—paste, sizing or dressing preparation
KLISTRING—sizing, dressing
KLOSS—bracket
KNÄBOM—knee beam
KNIPPE—cluster
KNIV—knife, blade
KNUT—knot
KNYTA—to tie
KNYTA FRAM VARPEN—to tie the warp to the cloth beam
KNYTNING—tying
KNYTNING AV SKAFT, TRAMPOR OCH LATTOR—tie-up of harnesses, treadles and lamms
KON—cone
KONFORMIG—conical
KONSTVÄVNAD—art weave
KONTRALATTA—contra-lamm
KONTRAMARSCH—contramarch, contramarch loom, independent action loom
KONTROLL AV UPPSÄTTNINGEN —check of loom set-up
KONTROLLERA—to check

KONTURLINJE—contour line, outline
KONTURTRÅD—contour thread, out-line thread
KORNDRÄLL—type of diamond twill
KORSKYPERT—cross twill
KORSSPOLE—cross-wound spool
KORT—card
KORTKEDJA—card chain
KORTLATTA—short lamm
KORTSLAGNING—card punching, card perforating
KORTVALS—card cylinder
KRABBASNÅR—inlay technique with pattern diagonal in character
KRAMA, KLÄMMA—to squeeze, press
KRAPP—madder
KRÄPPBINDNING—crêpe weave
KROK—hook
KROMFÄRGÄMNE—mordant dyes
KRYMPFRI—shrinkage resistant
KRYMPNING—shrinkage
KRUSA—to ruffle
KUDDÖVERDRAG—pillow cover
KUGG—cog
KUGGHJUL—cogwheel
KUVERT TABLETT—place mat
KVADRATISK SATIN—square satin weave
KVALITET—quality, structure, class, kind, grade
KVARTSBLEKT—quarter bleached
KVIST (I TRÄ)—knot (in wood)
KYPERTBINDNING—twill weave
KYPERTDRÄLL—twill *dräll*
KYPERTGRUNDBINDNING—basic twill
KYPFÄRGÄMNEN—vat dyes

LÄDERREM—leather strap, thong
LANG—bout, one complete circuit of the warp on the warping reel
LANGARN—linen floss
LANGETTSTYGN—buttonhole stitch
LÄNK—link
LÄNKA NER EN VARP—to make a warp chain
LANTRASFÅR—domestic sheep (Swedish)
LAPP—patch
LATTA—lamm
LÄTTA PÅ BROMSNINGEN—to release the brake
LIKA MYCKET—equally
LIKSIDIG—reversible
LIN—flax
LINBLAD—distaff
LINFRÖ—flax seed
LINGARN—linen yarn

LINGARN MED LÖS SNODD—slightly twisted linen yarn, floss
LINNEDUK—table linen
LJUSÄKTA FÄRG—light-fast color
LJUSBRUN—tan, light brown
LJUSVEKEGARN—cotton roving
LOCK—loop resembling half-heddle, used in damask weaving on draw-harness loom
LOD—weight, lingo
LODRÄT—perpendicular, vertical
LÖPARE—runner
LÖPMETER—linear meter
LÖS, GLAPPIG—loose, slack
LÖSTAGBAR—movable
LUCKA—aperture, slit
LUDDA UPP SIG—to nap
LUGG—nap, pile
LUGGIG, LUDEN—shaggy
LUT—lye

MAL—moth
MALSÄKER—moth proof
MANCHESTERSAMMET—corduroy
MÄNGD, ANTAL—quantity, number
MÄRKE, STRECK—mark, line
MARKIS—awning
MASKA—stitch, link or loop of yarn
MASKINVÄVD—machine woven, power loomed
MASKINVÄVSTOL—power loom
MÄTA—to measure
MATARHAKE—rachet, pawl
MATELASSÉ—quilting
MATT—dull
MÅTT—measurement, dimension
MATTA—mat
MATTA SOM TÄCKER HELA GOL-VET—carpet (wall-to-wall)
MATTA, MINDRE GOLVMATTA—rug
MATTSTICKA—stick shuttle
MEDELLÄGE—central position
MELLANRUM—space
METER—meter, equal to 39.37 inches. Abbr. *m*
METERVARA (YARDVARA)—yardage
METRISKT SYSTEM—metric system
MÖBELTYG—upholstery fabric
MÖGEL—mildew
MÖNSTER—pattern, design
MÖNSTERPARTI—pattern block
MÖNSTERYTA—pattern area
MONTERING AV VÄVSTOL—assem-bling of a loom
MOSSKRÄPP—mossy crêpe
MOTDRAG—counter balance
MOTSATSINSLAG—opposite weft
MOTSTÅ SMUTS—soil resistant

MULTIPLICERA—to multiply
MUNKABÄLTE—monk's belt
MUTTER—nut (metal)
MUTTERBRICKA—washer
MYGGTJÄLL—"mosquito netting," lace weave

NAGGAD—jagged, studded
NÅL—needle
NÄT—net
NATURSILKE—pure silk
NATURVIT—off-white
NOCK—pile, knot
NOPPA—loop, burl, knot
NÖTHÅRSGARN—yarn spun of 25% cow hair and 75% coarse wool
NUMMER—number
NYSTKRONA, NYSTVINDA—swift, skein holder, reel

OBÖJLIGT—unbending, rigid
ÖGLA—loop
ÖGLEKNUT—loop knot
ÖGLOR I ÄNDARNA PÅ ETT SNÖRE—cord with looped ends
OLIKSIDIG—non-reversible
OMKRETS—circumference
OMSLAGSPAPPER—wrapping paper
OMTRAMPNING—shifting treadles
OMVÄXLA—to alternate
ÖPPEN—open
ORNAMENT, SLINGA—decoration, scroll
OVANFÖR—above
ÖVERBINDNING—upper tie-up
ÖVERDEL—top member, cap, top castle
ÖVERDRAG—slip cover
ÖVERFÖRA—transpose
ÖVERHOPPAT RÖR—skipped dent
OVERKSAM—idle
ÖVERROCK—overcoat

PACKE, VARUBAL—package (of goods)
PACKE (TYGBUNT)—bolt (of cloth)
PALL—bench
PANAMA—basket weave
PARTI—block, group
PARTIINREDNING—block draft, short draft
PARTIMÖNSTER—block pattern
PASMA—a section of a skein of yarn. A skein, though wound in one continuous strand, is divided into several sections which are separated by the divisional skein string
PASMA TRÅD—divisional skein string
PATRONERING—drafting

PATRONTECKNARE—draftsman
PERSIENNER—Venetian blinds
PINNE, PLUGG—peg
PLOCKA IN—lay in, insert
PRESSNING—pressing
PRICK—dot
PROV, TYGPROV—swatch, sample
PRYDA—adorn
PUTSA, KLIPPA—to trim, clip
PUTSNING—trimming, clipping

RÅBANDSKNOP—square knot
RÅBREDD—raw width, width of fabric before finishing process
RAD—row
RÄKNESTICKA—slide rule
RAKT-ÖVER-SOLVNING—consecutive draft, plain draft, diagonal draft
RÅLÄNGD—raw length, length of the fabric before finishing process
RAND—stripe
RAND, BÅRD—stripe, border
RANDIG—striped
RAPPHÖNSÖGA—partridge eye twill pattern
RAPPORT—repeat
RÄT, RAK—straight
RÄTSIDA—face side, right side
RÅVÄV—raw fabric, fabric before finishing process
RAYONGARN—rayon yarn
RAYONULL—cut rayon
REDKAM—raddle
REDSKAP—implement, equipment
RELIEFFLOSSA—relief *flossa*
REM—strap
REMSA—strip
REN SPETSSOLVNING—single pointed threading
REP—rope
REPA UPP—unravel
REST—remainder
RESULTAT—result
RIBBA, STÅNG—lath, rod, bar
RIDDRÄKT—riding habit
RIPS—rep
RIPSMATTA—rep rug
RÖLAKAN—type of laid-in technique
RÖR—dent
ROSENGÅNG—rosepath
ROSENKRANSEN—rose wreath twill pattern
ROST—rust
ROTTING—rattan
RUGGA—to raise a nap, to tease
RULLE, BOBBIN—roller, spool
RULLE, KAVEL—roller
RULLJALUSI—window shade

RULLSTÄLLNING—spool rack
RUNDTVINNAT LINGARN—round-twisted linen yarn
RUNDVÄV—tube weave, circular weave
RUTA—check, square
RUTIG DUBBELVÄVNAD—checked double weave
RUTIG KYPERT—diamond twill
RUTIG VÄVNAD—plaid, checked fabric
RUTPAPPER—graph paper, squared paper
RUTRAD—row of squares
RYA—long pile
RYA MATTA—rug with spaced knots and long pile
RYALINJAL—*rya* rod
RYCKA—to pull, jerk
RYCKVERK—fly shuttle device
RYCKVERKSSKYTTEL—fly shuttle
RYNKA—wrinkle, fold
RYNKA—to pucker, gather
RYNKIG EFFEKT—puckered effect
RYNKNING—shirring, gathering

SADELMAKARGARN—sadler's yarn
SAFFRAN—saffron (yellow color)
SÅLLDRÄLL—M's and O's, poor man's huck
SAMMANBINDA—connect, join
SAMMANBINDNINGSPUNKT—stitching point
SAMMANBUNDEN DUBBELVÄV—stitched double weave
SAMMANDRAGA SIG—contract
SAMMANFLÄTA—interlace
SAMMANSATTA BINDNINGAR—combined weaves
SAMMANSTÄLLNING—combination
SAMMET—velvet
SAMTIDIGT—at the same time
SANDBOM—sand beam
SANDKRÄPP—sand crêpe
SÄNGÖVERKAST—coverlet, bedspread
SÄNKA—to lower, depress
SÄNKTA TRÅDARNA I SKÄLET—the floor of the shed
SATIN—satin, sateen (woven in cotton)
SATINBINDNING—satin weave
SÄTTA IHOP—to assemble
SAX—scissors
SCHACKMÖNSTER—chess pattern
SCHAL—stole, shawl
SEKTIONSVARPA—sectional warping reel
SEKTIONSVARPBOM—sectional warp beam
SELFAKTOR—self acting, mule spinning machine

SENNAHKNUT—Sennah knot
SERIE—series
SERVETT—napkin
SEXSIDIG—hexagonal
SIDENTYG—silk material
SIDOARMAR (PÅ SLAGBOM)—side swords (of beater)
SIDOSTÖD (PÅ VÄVSTOL)—side support (of a loom)
SILKE—silk
SITTBRÄDA—seat
SKAFT—harness, heddle frame, pair of heddle sticks with heddles
SKAFTHÅLLARE—harness holder
SKAFTSMASKIN—dobby machine
SKAFTRAM—heddle frame
SKAFTREGLERARE—harness adjuster
SKAFTRÖRELSE—shedding motion
SKÄKTA—to scutch
SKÄKTETRÄ, SKÄKTEKNIV—scutching knife
SKÄL (FÖR SKYTTELN)—shed
SKÄL (VID SKÄLSTICKORNA)—lease, cross (at lease sticks)
SKÄLBLAD—weaving sword, pick-up stick
SKÄLSTICKOR—lease sticks
SKÅRA—slot
SKÄRKRONA—warping mill
SKÄRNING (AV ETT TYGS YTA)—shearing, cutting (of surface of a fabric)
SKÄRP—belt
SKARP ANSLUTNING—cut, sharp cut
SKARV—seam, splice
SKED—reed
SKEDA—to reed, sley, thread through reed
SKEDKROK—reed hook
SKEDLAG—reed holder on loom beater
SKEDNING—sleying, reeding
SKEDRAND—streak, reed mark
SKEDTÄTHET—size or set of reed, closeness of dents in reed
SKICKLIGHET, KONSTFÄRDIGHET—skill
SKISS—sketch
SKJORTA—shirt
SKJORTTYG—shirting
SKRUV—screw
SKRUVA UPP—unscrew
SKRYNKLA—wrinkle
SKYTTEL—shuttle
SKYTTELBANA—shuttle race
SKYTTELLÅDA—shuttle box
SKYTTLA—to throw the shuttle
SLADDRIGT—sleazy
SLAG—beat, pick
SLAGBOM—beater, pick
SLAGBOM LAGRAD UPPTILL (NERTILL)—beater swung from above (below)

SLÄNDA—distaff
SLANGVÄV—tube weave
SLARVTJÄLL—inlay of short pieces of rags to form patterns in rag rug
SLÄT—plain
SLÄTVÄV—plain weave
SLINGERVÄVNAD, SPETSVÄVNAD —gauze weave, leno
SLIRA—to slide
SLITSTARK—long wearing, durable
SLÖJA—veil
SLÖJD—crafts, handiwork, arts and crafts
SLUTET SKÄL—closed shed
SLUTTANDE—slanting
SMAL—narrow
SMÄLTA—to melt, dissolve, fuse
SMUTS—dirt
SNÄCKHJUL—worm wheel
SNÄRJA—to interlock
SNILJA—chenille
SNILJEGARN—chenille yarn
SNILJEMATTA—twice woven rug, rug woven with chenille yarn
SNODD (HÅRD, NORMAL, LÄTT, LÖS)—twist (tight, medium, light, loose)
SNODD VID SPINNING—spinning twist
SNODD VID TVINNING—ply twist
SNÖRE—cord
SOLV—heddle
SOLVA—to thread, draw in
SOLVHANK—loop of the heddle
SOLVKROK—heddle hook
SOLVNING—threading, drawing in
SOLVNOTA—threading draft
SOLVÖGA—heddle eye
SOLVSKÄL—heddle shed (tapestry weaving)
SOUMAK—inlay technique characterized by back-stitching
SPÄNNA—to stretch
SPÄNNARE—stretcher, temple
SPÄNNING, VARP—warp tension
SPÄRRHAKE—pawl, ratchet
SPÄRRHJUL—ratchet wheel
SPETS (VÄVNAD)—lace (weave)
SPETSINREDNING—pointed draft
SPETSKYPERT—pointed twill, turned twill, zig-zag twill
SPIK—nail
SPINNA—to spin
SPINNDOSA—spinneret
SPINNROCK—spinning wheel, treadle wheel
SPJÄLA—stick
SPLITTRA—to split, splinter
SPOLE—shuttle bobbin, bobbin, spool
SPOLA—to wind on a spool
SPOLMASKIN—bobbin winder, spool winder

SPOLSPINNING—spool spun (with reference to rayon; the opposite of cake spun or pot spun)
SPORTKLÄDER—sport clothes
SPRICKA—crack
SPRINT—pin, peg, cotter pin
SPRÖT—beam sticks, laths, pick-up sticks
STAD—selvedge, selvage
STADIG—sturdy, firm
STÄLLNING, STÖD—frame, support
STÅLSOLV—wire heddle
STAMPVALKNING—fulling
STÅNG, RIBBA—bar, rod
STATIV—stand, frame (of a loom)
STELT (OM MÖNSTER)—stiff, stark, lacking in grace (with reference to a pattern)
STOPPNÅL—darning needle
STÖTDÄMPARE AV GUMMI—rubber bumper
STÖTTA, STAKE, STÖR—prop, stake, pole
STRAMALJ—open weave, lace weave
STUDSARE—picker (in fly shuttle device, the part which impels the shuttle through the warp)
STYCK—piece
STYCK FÄRGAD—piece-dyed
STYV—stiff, taut
SUBTRAHERA—to subtract
SURA FÄRGÄMNEN—acid dyes
SVEPA—to beam
SVEPA OM (PÅ NYTT)—to beam again
SVEPNING—beaming
SVETTHÄRDIGHET—fastness to perspiration
SYMMETRISK RAPPORT—balanced repeat
SYMMETRISK MÖNSTER—balanced pattern
SYNTETISKA FIBRER—synthetic fibers

TÄCKFAKTOR—covering factor
TAFT—taffeta
TAGA NER EN VÄV—to remove the weaving from the loom
TAPET, VÄVD—tapestry
TAPP — peg, tenon
TAPPHÅL—mortise
TÄTHET I SKEDEN—set in the reed, set of warp in the reed
TÄTRAND I VARP—close area in the warp
TÄTT INTILL—close to
TEKNIK, VÄV—technique, kind of weave
TEN—spindle, pin
TEXTUR—texture

TILLÄGG—addition
TILLSLAGNING—beating
TISTEL—teasel
TJOCK—thick
TOFS—tassel
TOMRÖR—empty dent
TORKA—to dry
TOTALA TRÅDANTALET—total number of threads in warp
TRÄ—wood
TRÅD—thread
TRÅDANTAL—number of threads, total number of warp threads
TRÅDGRUPP—group of threads
TRÅDLUCKA—slit, open space in a weave
TRÅDSYSTEM—set of warp and weft
TRAMPA—treadle, pedal
TRAMPA—to treadle
TRAMPA NER—to depress the treadle
TRAMPAD SOM SOLVAD—treadled as drawn in
TRAMPFÄSTE—bracket
TRAMPORDNINGSNOTA—treadling draft
TRAMPUPPKNYTNINGSMÖNSTER—treadle tie-up plan
TRÅNG—narrow, limited, crowded
TRÄNS—braid, ridge
TRASA—rag
TRASSLA SIG—to tangle
TREDUBBEL—triple, three fold, three ply
TRE-SKAFT KYPERT—drill
TRISSA, BLOCK—pulley
TRISSBRÄDE—pulley frame
TRUMMA—drum
TRYCKA—to print
TRYCKT MÖNSTER—printed design
TUNG—heavy
TUNN—thin
TUSKAFT, TVÅSKAFT—plain weave, tabby
TUSS, GARN—butterfly bobbin, finger bobbin, hand bobbin
TVÅLLÖSNING—soap suds
TVÄRRANDIG—horizontally striped
TVÄRSLÅ—crossbar
TVÅ SKAFT—two harnesses
TVÅSKAFT, TUSKAFT—plain weave, tabby
TVÅSKAFTINSLAG—tabby weft
TVÅTRÅDIG—two ply
TVÄTT—wash, laundry
TVÄTTA—to wash, launder
TVÄTTBAR—washable
TVÄTTHÄRDIG—washable
TVINNA—to ply, twist
TVINNGARN—ply yarn

TVIST—alternate dark and light wefts in a weft-faced weave giving an effect of vertical stripes
TYG—cloth, fabric
TYGBOM—cloth beam
TYGBOMSREGULATOR—automatic take-up motion
TYNGD—weight

UDDA OCH JÄMT—odd and even
ULL—wool
ULL AV BRA KVALITET—wool of good quality
ULL AV DÅLIG KVALITET—wool of poor quality
ULLFÄLL—fleece
ULLFÄRGAD—fleece-dyed wool
ULLFETT—wool fat, grease
ULLGARN—woolen yarn
ULLHÅR—hair wool
ULLKARDA—wool carder
ULLSORTERING—wool picking
ULLSPETS—britch wool
ULSTER—top coat, heavy woolen coat
ULSTERTYG—heavy coat material
UNDER—below
UNDERSIDA—wrong side, reverse side
UNDERSKÄLSLÄGE—warp in lowered position
UPPHÄMTA—technique woven with a weaving sword, draw device or draw-harness arrangement
UPPHÖJNING—ridge, raised area
UPPKNYTNING—tie-up
UPPKNYTNINGSMÖNSTER—tie-up plan
UPPSÄTTNING—setting up
URHOLKA—to hollow out
URHOLKNING—groove
UTBREDD—spaced
UTESLUTA—to exclude, omit
UTRUSTNING—equipment
UTSTÄLLNING—show, exhibition, display

VADDERA—to pad
VADDTÄCKE—quilt
VÅFFELVÄV—waffle weave
VÄFT—weft
VÅG (ATT VÄGA PÅ)—scales, weighing machine
VÄGGBONAD—wall hanging, tapestry
VÅGIG—wavy
VÅGRÄT—horizontal
VALKNING—milling, felting, fulling
VALKTVÄTTNING—scouring
VANLIG—ordinary, common

VÄNSTERSNODD—left-hand twist, s-twist

VÄRMEISOLERING—thermal insulation

VARP—warp

VARPA, VARPSTÄLLNING—warping reel, warping mill

VARPBOM—warp beam

VARPBRÄDA, VARPRAM—warping board

VARPFLOTTERING—warp float

VARPGARN—warp yarn

VARPKEDJA—warp chain

VARPKYPERT—warp-faced twill

VARPNING—warping

VARPORDNING—warp arrangement, warp plan,

VARPRIPS—warp-faced rep

VARPSATIN—warp satin, warp-faced satin

VARPSPÄNNING—tension of the warp

VARPSTÄLLNING—warping reel, warping mill

VARPSTICKA—paddle

VARPTÄTHET—ends per inch, set in the reed

VARPTRÅD—warp thread, end

VARPTRUMMA—drum on a warping mill

VARV—turn, revolution

VÄSKA—bag

VÄVA—to weave

VÄVD MED KASTSKYTTEL—woven with a throw shuttle, handwoven

VÄVD MED RYCKVERK—woven with a fly shuttle, hand loomed

VÄVERSKA—weaver (feminine)

VÄVFEL—error in weaving

VÄVKNUT—weaver's knot

VÄVNAD—weave, web

VÄVNOTA—draft

VÄVREDSKAP—weaving equipment

VÄVSKED—reed

VÄVSPÄNNARE—stretcher, temple

VÄVSTOL—loom

VÄVSTOL VID VILKEN VÄVAREN SITTER PÅ MARKEN MED FÖTTERNA I EN GROP—pit loom

VÄVSTUGA—weaving studio

VÄVUPPSÄTTNING—setting up the warp on the loom, dressing the loom

VÄXEL—gear

VÄXTFÄRGÄMNE—natural dyes, vegetable dyes

VECK—crease

VECK—pleat

VECKA—to crease

VECKA SIG—to fold, crease

VECKNING—pleating

VEPA—blanket, runner, wall hanging

VEV—crank, handle

VIKA—to fold

VIKT—weight

VIRKA—crochet

YIORDESKNUT—Ghiordes knot, also called *rya* knot

YLLE—woolen material

YTA—surface

This list is alphabetical to conform to English language . But in Swedish, words beginning with accented vowels would go at the end.

267

INDEX

R

S

T

Twill, multiple harness 69
Twill pattern, partridge eye 88
Twill, order 74
Twill, plaited 76, 84
Twill, pointed 76, 86
Twill, warp backed 164
Twill, wavy 85, 88
Twill, weft faced 164
Twist 69
Tying the contramarch 245

U

Unbleached 172
Upphämta 51, 145
Upholstery fabric 88, 106, 201

V

V-point 100
Velvet 209

W

Warp 9, 13, 49
Warp beam 24
Warp, binding 178
Warp bouts 18
Warp chain 16, 23
Warp, float 61
Warp, tension 43, 46
Warp, thrums 48
Warping reel 13
Warping reel sectional 13, 18
Weave, art 46, 51, 100
Weave, basic 50

Weave, basket 51, 61, 205, 228
Weave, checked 143
Weave composition 178
Weave, construction 49, 51
Weave, crackle 145
Weave, crêpe 116, 117
Weave, derivative 51
Weave, diagonal 118, 122
Weave, double 166
Weave, checked double 169
Weave, figured double 172
Weave, honeycomb 106, 107
Weave, lace 111, 114
Weave, laid-in 41
Weave, multi-harness 41
Weave, stitched double 175
Weave, tabby 50, 56
Weave, tapestry 194
Weave, tube 166
Weave, twill 50, 65
Weave, waffle 110
Weaves combined 121
Weaves, interlocked 186
Weaving sword 131, 132
Weft 41, 49
Weft, float 68, 185
Weft skip 44
Whipcord 74
Wool 205
Work sheet 231

Y

Yarn, boucle 63
Yarn calculation 224
Yarn, worsted 234
Yarn, Z twist weft 69